D0835287

The Easy Burden of Pleasing God

PATTY KIRK

IVP Books

An imprint of InterVarsity Press
Downers Grove, Illinois

InterVarsity Press
P.O. Box 1400, Downers Grove, IL 60515-1426
World Wide Web: www.ivpress.com
Email: email@ivpress.com

InterVarsity Press® is the book-publishing division of InterVarsity Christian Fellowship/
USA®, a movement of students and faculty active on campus at hundreds of universities,
colleges and schools of nursing in the United States of America, and a member movement of
the International Fellowship of Evangelical Students. For information about local and
regional activities, write Public Relations Dept., InterVarsity Christian Fellowship/USA,
6400 Schroeder Rd., P.O. Box 7895, Madison, WI 53707-7895, or visit the IVCF website at
<www.intervarsity.org>.

All Scripture quotations, unless otherwise indicated, are taken from THE HOLY BIBLE,
NEW INTERNATIONAL VERSION®, NIV® Copyright © 1973, 1978, 1984, 2011 by Biblica,
Inc.™ Used by permission. All rights reserved worldwide.

While all stories in this book are true, some names and identifying information in this book
have been changed to protect the privacy of the individuals involved.

Design: Cindy Kiple
Images: illustration of bird and plants: © AnnaPaff/iStockphoto
Interior design: Beth Hagenberg

ISBN 978-0-8308-4303-9

Printed in the United States of America ∞

A catalog record for this book is available from the Library of Congress.

P	18	17	16	15	14	13	12	11	10	9	8	7	6	5	4	3	2	1
Y	28	27	26	25	24	23	22	21	20	19	18	17	16	15	14	13

Contents

Preface

IN ALL THE JOBS I'VE HAD, most women I've worked with have figured out when they're going to retire. They know the exact date, without having to tot it up when you ask them. Perhaps my male colleagues know their retirement dates too, but it's the women who talk about retiring. They fantasize about it—fantasies I call jobicidal ideation, the primary symptom of an illness whose name I have not yet invented. It's a common illness. Perhaps the most common of our culture.

Once, at a retreat with other professional women, I mentioned a sick fantasy I have about lying in a hospital bed, rendered suddenly stress-free by cancer or paralysis or some other act of God.

Probably some of these women are struggling with loved ones laid low by illness, it occurred to me as I spoke, and I was regretting my words even as they emerged from my mouth. I often do this. Especially under stress.

But my listeners' response surprised me. They nodded. Vigorously. Several women present said they'd had exactly the same fantasy. The hospital bed. The silence. The IV drip sustaining one effortlessly. Visits from family and friends only during visiting hours. The hushed messages of encouragement.

Perhaps the stress of reconciling life's many demands—jobs, keeping the house pleasant, parenting, worrying everything into place—isn't about gender. After all, men have been working and living in houses and parenting simultaneously for centuries. I once read, though, that working women, in contrast to working men, typically lunch at their desks, still working. Or else they don't eat at all. I have noticed this is true of most women I know. I often walk in on female colleagues gnawing away at a health bar while working, and there are typically several female students who bring food to my classes so they can rush off to their next class or meeting or study session without wasting any time at a table. We women can't stop working or studying or doing long enough to join our male peers in the cafeteria and eat a decent meal.

I also don't see my female coworkers or students walking around campus with gym bags, as my male coworkers and students often do. A few women do work out, of course. Some give up that hurried desk-lunch to fit in aerobics or body pump. Others get up in darkness to attend an early morning workout. I know because I've been there. Although the workouts were open to both sexes, male participants were so rare we made jokes about the odd one who showed up, half-awake, to join us, young and old, in our leggings and oversized T-shirts, lunging and panting together through driving songs about power: "What's Love Got to Do with It?" and an irritatingly compelling song about being a hero that I'd find myself singing as I rushed to class afterward and then to a core curriculum meeting and then back to my office. By then I'd be starving, so I'd microwave some popcorn to eat as I coached a student through an essay or graded papers or prepared class for the next day.

For a long time I thought my own stress was simply the monstrous product of doing too much. And surely it was. At the time of that retreat, I was not only a full-time mom with a full-time teaching job but also trying to help my husband transition out of farming through more schooling and into a new career. Our weekends were taken up with farm chores, Kris's homework, my grading, our daughters' ball games and school projects, church activities.

Such a life *is* stress, I reasoned. So I gritted my mouth into a grin. And I bore it.

Just making time for that retreat in the first place had taken some effort—although, with a widowed mother-in-law living on our farm eager to feed everyone and look after Charlotte and Lulu whenever Kris and I were too busy, I was luckier than many. Even so, convincing myself to take a break from my responsibilities for a work-free weekend of prayer and fellowship seemed impossible. Wrong even. I felt guilty for unloading everything onto Kris and his mom. I was sure I wouldn't be able to find anyone to help run children's church in my stead. And I would inevitably return, I knew, so overwhelmed by essays still to be graded and a house that had to be put back the way I like it that I would instantly become the version of myself I liked least: one who snapped at her husband, was distracted with her children, bulldozed through class lessons and office hours, raced home to make dinner, and couldn't stop, not even for a minute, to unwind. Or reflect. Or smile.

Once, when Lulu was still just little, she drew up a list of behavioral commandments for the woman I became at such times. I was to look her in the face when she addressed me. I was not to sigh or say *uh-hm*. I was to put down whatever I was doing. A woman whose small daughter has to take such measures is not who God wants her to be, that much I knew, and the desire to transform myself into something better—a less distracted mother, a more loving wife, a calmer teacher, a more faithful and obedient child of God—weighed heavily on me. Thus, the stress to get it all done— not to mention the attendant guilt when I didn't get it all done, as I inevitably didn't—infected not just my professional and relational responsibilities but my spiritual work-life as well.

I was relatively new to faith in those days, having grown up believing the basic gospel but then plummeted into unbelief in my
teens. When, after decades of yearning, I rediscovered God in my
midthirties, I had my spiritual work cut out for me. What had been
so easy as a child—little more than an awareness of God, watching
me, listening to me, loving me—seemed so much more challenging
in adulthood. The workload of the believer advertised in church
and among my Christian friends was intricate and consuming.
Bible studies and Sunday school classes. Mission work. Charity
work. Children's church and Vacation Bible School and other
church responsibilities. Prayer groups and prayer journals and
prayer lists. Morning devotions. Daily Bible reading.

Not to mention all the behavioral commands filling the Bible.
Not just the Big Ten but hundreds of lesser ones from Jesus
himself. Love not only one's friends and family but one's enemies.
Go out and make disciples of the world. Give everything to the
poor and follow him. I knew all about these behavioral expectations of Christians, even though as a new believer I was actually
reading the Bible—sitting down and really studying it, not merely
musing on the little snippets of it read aloud during a service—for
the first time. I knew my salvation didn't depend on my fulfillment
of any commandments—or, in fact, on anything I did or didn't
do—but there they all were, filling the pages of Old Testament and
New: rules pertaining to one's relationships and money and food
and worship, to how one dressed and wore one's hair, to emotions
and illnesses and mildew management, rules even about one's attitudes toward these rules.

And there was Jesus himself proclaiming that, "until heaven and
earth disappear, not the smallest letter, not the least stroke of a pen,
will by any means disappear from the Law until everything is accomplished" (Matthew 5:18). Wherever I looked in Scripture, living
by faith seemed to be all about getting things accomplished. Doing
God's work seemed an onerous and never-ending undertaking.

But, I discovered, the Bible was also full of promises about the pleasurable nature of God's work. Key among them are the Old Testament's recurrent promises that leading a life of faith results in contentment and longevity and the New Testament's promises that Jesus' yoke is easy, that his burden is light—that, indeed, the work of God is merely a matter of listening to and believing in Jesus.

So, as I slipped and slid around trying to find my spiritual feet and make my way God-ward, I was increasingly struck by the disparity between those comforting promises of ease, on the one hand, and all those crushing rules. Loving others seemed no light burden, to me. Nor did turning the other cheek when I was angry or dipping into my nearly nonexistent resources of money and time to help out others in need.

Worse, the interior yoke of my own secret striving was anything but easy. *Why am I not better at praying?* I worried. *Or parenting? Or spousing or neighboring, for that matter? Shouldn't I be spending more time with my elderly relatives? And how does one make oneself cheerful in one's charitable work?*

I'm a how-to kind of person. I hate being told to "just" do something, such as "Only believe" or "Just let go and let Jesus," without explanation of how to go about it.

"How do I 'just' give my problems to Jesus'?" I wailed to my Christian friends and mentors from my first moments as an adult believer. "How does one *do* that?"

In this book, I attempt to answer my own questions about living the life of faith. How, exactly, does one go about doing God's work? And, if God's work *is* merely to believe in Jesus, why does it seem so much more complicated and demanding—another set of overwhelming job requirements on top of all my other responsibilities? Finally, and most importantly, how precisely does one go about experiencing Jesus' yoke as easy, his burden as light?

This book is at once an examination of Scripture's invitation to take Jesus' yoke upon us and find rest for our souls and a playbook, from my own life, of what doing so might look like. The Bible has much to say on the nature of our spiritual work assignments, and I visit and often revisit key biblical stories in the course of the book. I scrutinize Scripture especially closely for help in reconciling the calls to serve and sacrifice and even to suffer in the name of God with God's many promises of ease, contentment, rest. I also experiment with taking Jesus at his word by making ease and enjoyment major goals in any spiritual work assignment.

I like to break jobs into tasks that I can define before I undertake them. It makes the work seem more doable, more manageable, less daunting. In writing books, for example, nothing gives me more confidence than drawing up a book proposal in which I divvy my message into a tidy list of titled chapters. And in teaching writing, I really have no idea what to do before I have written a syllabus.

Not just a syllabus. A SYLLABUS. My syllabi—which I admit are mocked by my colleagues and some of my students and even by some saner and more relaxed part of myself buried down beneath the worry about things not getting accomplished—are detailed forecasts of every topic that could come up in the course, every day's activities, every assignment, every potential problem. I construct my syllabi as web pages into which all my course documents are linked: writing inventories, brainstorming aids, grammar and punctuation checklists, examples of good writing, troubleshooting worksheets, and, most importantly, fully fleshed-out instructions for each assignment.

I feel secure in having such a plan for the semester. I know *exactly* what my students and I are going to do on a given day. (Or, at least, I think I do.) And my students know *exactly* what's due when and *exactly* how to do it. (Or so I believe, until I find out otherwise.)

Very precise and exhaustive syllabi have a drawback, though.

When we run out of time for some task—and we *will* run out of time—I will get stressed out and feel that I have failed. And my students will get stressed out and *know* that I have failed. And the whole semester will go temporarily awry until I somehow find time, usually during the mid-semester onslaught of grading, to re-teach myself how I constructed my online syllabi in the first place and then fix everything to my and my students' satisfaction—which is to say to no one's satisfaction, since by this time we're all not only stressed and confused but wedded to the original plan just as amorously as writers are wedded to their first drafts.

Sometimes I "crossing-guard on." I mean this metaphor in the sense of "soldier on," but I want you to get an image of the impossibility of orderliness in this task, despite my orange vest and air of authority, with kids running every which way and brakes shrieking and nothing being quite as safe and predictable as I would like my courses to be. Sometimes, as I say, I march forth into that new syllabus, and my students and I jerk to the end of the semester still following some sort of plan, however tenuously. Other times I throw it all in and wing it from mid-semester onward. Either way, I will know that I have wrecked the course, and the students will confirm this when they write on their course evaluations that I "chased rabbits" or "seemed disorganized."

All this to say that this book will offer some examples of how one *might* make God's work more manageable, pleasurable, successful, and, above all, guilt-free and stress-free. However, I do not want to give anyone the mistaken idea that I am prescribing certain behaviors or that I think a Christian is someone who struggles through the business of faith in exactly the same way I do. I am saying, in fact, the opposite.

This book is, in other words, *not* one of my syllabi, and I do not want you to enter into it as my students and I do my syllabi. Do not wed yourself to what I write or try to mimic my behaviors. Rather, let my stories, struggles, and research inspire you to come up with your own way of taking Jesus at his word, your own way of allowing him to pull the plow through your rocky soil, your own way of believing ever more deeply in the exhilarating reality of his presence there beside you, doing it all.

PART 1

God's Great Promises
of Ease

1

Love Versus Rules

"I am the LORD your God, who brought
you out of Egypt, out of the land of slavery.
You shall have no other gods before me.
You shall not make for yourself an image in the form
of anything in heaven above or on the earth beneath or in the
waters below. You shall not bow down to them or worship
them; for I, the LORD your God, am a jealous God."

EXODUS 20:2–5

WHEN, AS A NEW BELIEVER, I BEGAN reading the Bible for myself, I was struck from the start by the tender picture of God presented there. Contrary to my preconceptions, Yahweh of Genesis was given to "walking in the garden in the cool of the day" (Genesis 3:8) and interacting as any fond parent might with the creatures he had created. He conversed with them. He brought the animals to Adam "to see what he would name them" (Genesis 2:19). To my surprise, the author of the Ten Commandments and eventual perpetrator of the Flood and other Old Testament atrocities I found disturbing did not come across to me as a rule-giving despot from a remote era and culture or as a supreme power utterly incomprehensible to humans but as a real person, with recognizable and contemporary and very human-seeming habits and emotions.

Indeed, forgive my irreverence, but God reminded me a lot of myself. As a new mom with a newborn and a toddler, I was experiencing both the joys and the miseries of parenthood, learning as I went. One moment my girls were cuddly and affectionate, trying to outdo me in a game of "How much do you love me?" (Lulu always won with her bizarre avowal, invented in babyhood, "I love you as much as the world loves itself!") The next moment they were throwing tantrums about nothing or refusing to do some small task I had given them or fighting each other with a viciousness only a onetime sibling could believe possible. (Charlotte was a biter; Lulu gouged with her long nails.)

To the parent I was then, God sounded like a fellow parent. From the beginning, he was clearly as enthused about parenthood as I was. He had designed the perfect nursery for his humans—a lovely garden full of cute animals! He organized companionship for them—playdates! And he arranged a host of fun activities with which they could occupy themselves: digging in the garden, gathering fruits from the trees, lording it over the animals, giving them names. What could be more delightful for a child?

Just as I did for my daughters, God had high hopes for the humans he had created. He clearly expected them to enjoy the delightful existence he had created for them and to return his love and was understandably devastated when they didn't. Within the first few pages of our human childhood, we humans were breaking God's one rule—a protective rule, it seemed to me, very much akin to my own "Don't touch the stove or it'll burn you!" or "If you hurt someone, you have to say you're sorry!"—and increasingly taking credit for and even trying to outdo God's creative triumphs. Upon the birth of Cain, Eve barely acknowledges God's part in this miracle, and only a few chapters later Abram and Sarai try to orchestrate for themselves the countless offspring God has promised them by having Abram sleep with their servant Hagar.

The humans even seek to "uncreate" one another through murder. When Cain gets so jealous of his brother that he wants to kill him, God reasons with him—"Why are you angry? Why is your face downcast? If you do what is right, will you not be accepted?" (Genesis 4:6–7)—sounding exactly as I know I have, reasoning with Charlotte and Lulu engaged in one of their battles. To no avail, in each scenario.

In response to human violence, the God of all creation, we're told, "was deeply troubled" (Genesis 6:6). Other translations are more poignant: "It grieved him at his heart" (KJV). "It broke his heart" (NLT, *The Message*). And, in a translation I find especially moving, "his heart was filled with pain" (NIV 1984). I could certainly identify with that parental feeling.

The myriad rules of Scripture seemed, as I progressed through the Old Testament that first time, to derive from these developments, just as, in my own family, my daughters' misdeeds generally occasioned new rules, a trend initiated in part by the girls' decree, jointly conceived in early childhood, that my husband and I were not allowed to get mad at or punish them for offenses—such as taking off all their clothes to go roll in a mud puddle with our dogs—that had not been specifically designated as forbidden beforehand. After the mud puddle incident, which resulted in their both being covered in a prickly red rash, we banned not only mud puddle bathing but all public nudity and any dog-inspired activities that had not been checked out in advance. God's increasingly rule-driven interaction with his children seemed similarly inspired.

Even God's rules, though, to the amateur believer I was in those days, sounded intimate and loving. Consider the opening words of the Ten Commandments:

"I am the LORD your God, who brought you out of Egypt, out
of the land of slavery.

You shall have no other gods before me.

You shall not make for yourself an image in the form of
anything in heaven above or on the earth beneath or in the
waters below. You shall not bow down to them or worship
them; for I, the LORD your God, am a jealous God, punishing
the children for the sin of the parents to the third and fourth
generation of those who hate me, but showing love to a
thousand generations of those who love me and keep my
commandments." (Exodus 20:2–6)

God offers these commands very much in the context of his love
for them. He rescued them from slavery, he reminds them. He's
jealous of their affections. He will punish those who are hateful, he
warns, but he enthusiastically shows love to those who love him—
and even to their future descendants.

Though rarely referred to as "Father" at all in the Old Testament
except in a few metaphorical-sounding phrases in Isaiah and Jeremiah, the Yahweh of the first few books of Scripture is clearly our
actual *father*, who engendered us and, from the very beginning, sincerely loved us and longed to spend time with us. A parent with the
fondest of hopes for us, who suffered bitterly when we returned his
gentleness with violence and his love with hatred. A heartbroken
parent whose driving desire, it seemed to me, was to be loved back.

Substitute *Father*—or, even better, something more like *Abba*,
the Aramaic equivalent of *Daddy* that Jesus used to address his
Father—for the less approachable-sounding "God" and "LORD" in
the first two commandments, and you will get a feeling for the
deity I came to know when I read those first books of the Bible as
a new believer:

"I am Daddy, *your* daddy, who brought you out of Egypt, out
of the land of slavery.

You shall have no other daddies before me.

You shall not make for yourself an image in the form of anything in heaven above or on the earth beneath or in the waters below. You shall not bow down to them or worship them; for I, Daddy, *your* daddy, am a jealous daddy."

I, Father, your father, am a jealous father. Think of it: This is the Creator of heaven and earth addressing us. So plaintively. So like any parent, wanting to be loved best of all.

Nevertheless, God's children responded to his affection with hatred and violence from the earliest days, and we have continued to hate him by hurting one another—our siblings, fellow children of God!—ever since, often refusing even to acknowledge, much less appreciate, this Parent who aches with love for us. We have broken, and continue to break, God's heart. And all of Scripture testifies to our wrecked relationship with our Father and his resolution to repair it by sending himself in human form, not only as a sacrifice for our sins but also as a living model of the only behavioral requirement God had for us all along: love.

Despite its seemingly endless register of rules to be followed, the Bible, as I see it, is actually not so much a legal code as a love story, relating the account of the humans' wrecked relationship with their Father and his brokenhearted determination to fix it. The rules of Scripture are just a tiny part of that story.

Hopefully, my daughters do not regard the rules I've given them as they've matured—don't touch the stove, don't cross the street without looking, don't get a tattoo, don't do drugs, don't have sex with someone you barely know, don't engender babies you don't intend or have the resources to love and rear—and their own dutiful avoidance of such behaviors as the main business of our relationship. If they did, then they would think my love for them less if ever they failed—as they inevitably will fail in at least some of the charges I have put before them—and any interaction between us would be hopelessly encumbered by my unmet expectations and their probable feelings of guilt.

Rather, the work of our relationship—and, let me assure you, my relationship with my daughters, like all relationships, takes work on both their part and my own—amounts to acknowledgment and appreciation of one another, regular and honest communication, trustworthiness, and remorse when we fail. Though I would be delighted if my daughters obeyed my commands in every instance, the fact that they won't and haven't does not diminish my love for them in the slightest. Indeed, perverse as it may sound, their mistakes and corresponding expressions of remorse—and my own—have deepened our love over the years, I think. The job of loving them, for me, has entailed little more than spending time with them, believing in their potential, hoping them into healthy relationships of their own, and doing whatever it takes to restore our love when things go awry. Returning my love, for their part, looks much the same: being present themselves, believing that I have their best interests at heart, and willingly reconciling when necessary.

That's the work God expects from us. Love: the same work we expect of our own children. Nothing less. And not one jot, not one tittle more.

2

God's Work

Then they asked him,
"What must we do to do the works God requires?"
Jesus answered, "The work of God is this:
to believe in the one he has sent."

JOHN 6:28–29

❧

WE DON'T GENERALLY THINK OF LOVE AS WORK. Or as a skill that can be acquired or lost. Instead, we think of it as an emotion, like anger or sadness, that just comes upon us. We either feel love for someone, or else we don't. As a result of such an understanding of God's primary task for us, we rarely examine our own progress— or more typically, in my case, regress—in the business of love. But if love is the work God expects of us, it's instructive, I think, to consider what this work does and doesn't look like.

My daughters are fairly loving these days, as teenagers go. That is to say, their affections follow the mysterious schedule of their adolescent moods and whims. I generally have to wheedle and bribe them to pick up their rooms or bring in their dirty dishes from in front of the television, where I just served them a leisurely weekend breakfast while they watched *Star Wars* for the millionth time. Sometimes, to speed things up and avoid upsetting them, I just do myself whatever I wanted of them, dashing in and seizing their syrupy plates while they scowl and duck their heads around me, unwilling to miss the smallest detail of the riveting scene of Luke Skywalker fiddling with the engine of his flying car on some desert planet. And, although both daughters are good-natured and affectionate as a rule, their love often seems unduly driven by their desires. When they want something, they become positively lovable, sailing into my workspace to sit on my lap and pet me and thus prepare me for their request, but are instantly surly if I say no to their demands.

My daughters, in other words, would say they love me—they've even told me on occasion that I'm their favorite person in the world—and I cherish these sentiments. But I remember a time when their love was something altogether different: when they savored my nearness for nearness' sake and their only desire was to be held in my arms. Charlotte, before she was walking, would duck down her head and pretend to bump it on the floor so that I would rush over and pick her up. I have it on tape. And part of Lulu's putting-to-bed ritual, which lasted well into her school years, was something called "getting in my cupboard": I would fold myself around her body and croon her favorite childhood song, "The Holly and the Ivy," which I sang first in the happy major key tune and then, as her breathing thickened into sleep, in the slower minor version. Often, I fell asleep myself and lurched awake hours later to find my arm numb beneath her dream-weighted form and the house silent and dark.

My daughters' love nowadays is a selfish sort of love. They feel entitled to, not grateful for, my provision, and are outraged when my own expressions of love—such as saying no, surely one of my heaviest tasks as a parent—don't suit them.

They have the kind of love Jesus was talking about, I think, when he said to the hungry, violent, demanding crowds that followed him everywhere, "Very truly I tell you, you are looking for me, not because you saw the signs I performed but because you ate the loaves and had your fill" (John 6:26).

This is the scene of that remark: It's almost Passover, a hectic time in the Jewish year. Jesus has crossed to the far side of the Sea of Galilee followed by "a great crowd of people"—men alone numbering five thousand—who've seen "the signs he had performed by healing the sick" (John 6:2). Many are probably sick themselves and are following after Jesus because they want to be healed. After Jesus feeds them fish and bread from a little boy's lunch basket, they declare, "Surely this is the Prophet who is to come into the world" (John 6:14), and then set about forcing him to be their king.

There's lots of turmoil in this story—the rowdy followers, a brewing storm, the worried disciples trying to figure out how to manage everything—and Jesus keeps trying to get off by himself, first disappearing alone into the mountains, then walking out across the roiling waters of the Sea of Galilee. But the crowds and his disciples eventually find him again, and it is then that he chastises their sort of love, the kind motivated by the meal he has provided, the sick he has healed, the magic tricks they've heard about that they hope to witness with their own eyes. They have love that wants something.

That's not the kind of love God wants, Jesus says. Not love borne of hunger or pain or the desire to be entertained.

His words appall them, I'm guessing. After all, the feeding of the five thousand wasn't their idea, but his. And weren't they following after him in the first place precisely *because* they "saw the signs" he complains that they ignored?

"Do not work for food that spoils, but for food that endures to eternal life," Jesus goes on to counsel (John 6:27), and they are surely mystified. *What does he mean? What is this work one is expected to do to win eternal life? What in the world is it that God wants of us?* they finally ask.

Jesus' response is simple and uncharacteristically clear: "The work of God is this: to believe in the one he has sent" (John 6:29).

Or is it that clear? For the first many years of my adult faith, I understood Jesus' words to mean that there *was* no work of God. God did all the work required for us to have eternal life by sending Jesus to pay for our sins, so there was nothing left for us to do. And, indeed, that is how this passage is often taught. Whole theologies are anchored by this interpretation of Jesus' words.

Lately, though, I've come to understand Jesus' directive somewhat differently. It is not that we have *no* work to do to win God's approval. Rather, we have an important job before us: namely, to believe in the One God Sent—which I like to think of as Jesus' special name for himself. The work of God, he tells the crowds, is believing in him—that is, faith itself. And, as with all work, faith takes effort.

It was initially difficult for me to think of faith as the result of human effort, having experienced my own effortless restoration of the faith I had lost in adolescence. My rediscovery of God seemed to result from no work whatsoever on my own part but rather a series of God-manufactured miracles: putting in my way a believing husband, a house full of Bibles, a lifelong desire for the certainties I had enjoyed in childhood, and numerous friends and acquaintances eager to help me into heaven. Although I had been trying to believe for quite some time, the moment of my conversion—and it was a moment, not the gradual awareness that some believers experience—came upon me abruptly, when I wasn't looking for it to happen, having shortly before consciously given up on some hypothetical deity's ever doing anything to address the longing that filled me.

My ability to believe in the One God Sent, my sudden

awareness that the stories I had been reading and hearing—God existed, became one of us, died so that I could live forever—were not just edifying but true, my ability to believe such absurdities at all was a miracle, plain and simple. Utterly independent of my own efforts.

So, it has been an odd progress in my thinking to where I am now: the belief that faith itself takes effort on our part, the effort of taking Jesus at his word. The work of God, I have come to believe Jesus is saying, is to believe in him. To believe him when he says our all-powerful Father is unwilling to lose us despite our failures. To believe him when he says that belief is all that is expected of us and all we need. To believe him when he says that his yoke is easy and his burden light.

And it's difficult to believe Jesus in these matters, hence the Church's historic preoccupation with Christian conduct, the antithesis of Jesus' message. No matter how convinced a church may be that salvation cannot be earned, the sermons preached there are likelier to be about correct and incorrect behavior than about anything else. And few faith-hungry believers will feel fed unless they come away on Sunday with a plan of action, a renewed fervor to do something good or quit doing something bad.

The work of believing in the One God Sent takes, first off, the enormous effort of relinquishing something many of us prize more than anything else: our competing belief in ourselves. We have to convince ourselves that we can't shape our own lives but must trust the incredible promises that God *will* provide and *wants* us to be happy and has wonderful plans for us. Such trust takes effort, especially when our lives go awry.

Increasingly, I see my job as a believer as the conscious and often strangely reluctant return to my babyhood as a God-lover. To simultaneously give up control and give in to the unbelievable knowledge that I am loved, independent of my strivings and failures, independent of my ability to please, independent of my own love, amazingly enough. Only then am I able to do that simple, clear work of believing that has been assigned to me: to allow myself, like a baby, to be held and loved and, thus effortlessly, to give back love in return.

3

The One Command of the One God Sent

*"If you keep my commands, you will remain in my love,
just as I have kept my Father's commands and remain in his
love. I have told you this so that my joy may be in you and
that your joy may be complete. My command is this:
Love each other as I have loved you."*

JOHN 15:10–12

FOR A YEAR OR SO BEFORE I BECAME a believer, my husband and I regularly attended a Sunday school class called the "Old Marrieds." It was a rowdy class, made up of zealous misfits who had either been kicked out of other Sunday school classes or else had left in a huff over some matter of doctrine. One class member questioned what he called the "eternal security of the believer," a mystifying concept the rest of the class furiously defended. Another member, convinced that only the King James Version of the Bible was God-breathed—he objected even to the word *trans-*

lation used in reference to Scripture—kept leaving our class, then returning in despair of ever finding a group that shared his view. Whenever anyone read from another version, which was most of the time, he would grimace and squirm in his chair. Yet another class member insisted that whatever God or Jesus said to any specified listener—such as Cain or Jesus' disciples or Paul or the people of Jerusalem—was meant for that specified audience only, not for subsequent Bible readers like us.

One jolly couple regularly interrupted the theological debates to invite us all to their hot tub that evening—comic relief on any topic remotely related to, as another class member reverently pronounced the deity's name, Gaaaawwwwd, a being inspiring openmouthed awe in no one so much as me in those days. Although I didn't yet believe the stories we studied each week to be true, I was mightily impressed by them and longed for the God at their center. Possibly the best argument for the existence of a supernatural choreographer of the cosmos for me in those days was the weekly assembly of such a disparate assortment of people, all claiming to share the same faith.

They were, as I always mishear Johnny Cash singing in his gravelly version of "When the Roll Is Called Up Yonder," "the saved diverse": doctrinally opposed zealots united by a mysterious sameness of belief somehow gleaned, they all assured me, from the Bible's weird miscellany. Each one was as certain as the next of being on that other shore when the roll was called. Everyone regarded everyone else as in some degree apostate. Only later did I realize that, as the only actual atheist among them (perhaps the only atheist they had ever met), I myself was a key cohesive element of the class. Whatever their differences, they became as one—truly, the Church—in their shared passion to, as they said, "get me saved."

Toward that end, we systematically rooted through the Bible for its most essential messages: that God made us and loved us and suffered our rejection and, most importantly, had a plan to win us back. We read the Pentateuch, the Gospel of John, a few of

Paul's letters. By the time we got partway through Hebrews, I was a goner. I believed that God was my Father and his 100 percent divine Son my 100 percent human brother, eager to assist me into life eternal, and that the only contribution expected of me was my mustard-seed-sized faith—nay, merely my poor, doubt-fraught hope, according to Hebrews 11:1 and my exultant classmates—that the whole business was true.

Nevertheless, the fervently defended additional beliefs of my spiritual brothers and sisters continued to niggle me and significantly bolstered my doubt-life. Why, if salvation required nothing beyond belief in the One God Sent, did so many believers seem to have their own additional requirements? Were some of these diverse believers who had gotten me saved in fact wrong, seriously wrong, in their conflicting instructions about what was required to live a godly life? Were *they* the false teachers warned of throughout the Bible? Or, had God come up with a new set of requirements that I hadn't yet gotten to in my study of Scripture?

Requirements not in the Bible vexed me. Was salvation only *initially* based on faith alone but afterward on a new laundry list of dos and don'ts? Worse, why did I myself have the lingering notion that more was required that mere belief? As I staggered into faith after decades of effortless unbelief, I worried about the scary demonstrations of devotion I was sure God was about to demand of me.

Such as not being embarrassed by my newfound faith, for one. Jesus clearly stipulated, "Whoever is ashamed of me and my words, the Son of Man will be ashamed of them when he comes in his glory" (Luke 9:26).

And then there's the scary passage where Jesus rails against people who *think* they're safe but evidently aren't: "Not everyone who says to me, 'Lord, Lord,' will enter the kingdom of heaven, but only the one who does the will of my Father who is in heaven. Many will say to me on that day, 'Lord, Lord, did we not prophesy in your name and in your name drive out demons and in your name perform many miracles?' Then I will tell them plainly, 'I never knew you. Away from me, you evildoers!'" (Matthew 7:21–23). I might believe in the One God Sent, as these benighted miracle-workers apparently did, but maybe, if I didn't get it just right—if, because of something I did or didn't do, Jesus didn't know me somehow—I might suffer the same gnashing rejection.

In my childhood faith, back before the unpleasant oblivion of atheism sank over me and obliterated God from my view, I intuited God demanded great sacrifice and arduous effort from believers—nothing short of a life of abject holiness, like that of Father Damien, who ministered to people suffering from leprosy on Molokai until he contracted the disease himself and died of it.

If I returned to faith, I suspected as an adult, God might give me a similar assignment, some way of making good on my youthful adventures abroad. *Any day now*, I fretted as I took my first baby steps as a Christian, *I'll get the call to drop everything—job, house, our meager savings, my hard-won stability—and move back to Berlin or Beijing to convert my former friends and colleagues to faith in the One True God.*

My worries along these lines were borne out when my Sunday school class got to the story of the eager young rich guy who runs up to Jesus wanting to know how to earn eternal life. Jesus first asks if the guy obeys the commandments and lists a few of them. Then, after the man enthusiastically declares that he has obeyed them all his whole life, Jesus recommends that he give everything he has to the poor and follow him. The man goes away sad—because of his great wealth, we're told—and Jesus comments that it's "easier for a camel to go through the eye of a needle than for someone who is rich to enter the kingdom of God" (Matthew 19:24; see also Mark 10:25 and Luke 18:25).

The initial focus of my Sunday school class's ensuing discussion was the disparity between what was expected of *this* rich man versus another eager rich man we had already read about: the short tax collector Zacchaeus, who famously climbed a sycamore tree to see Jesus better.

"Look, Lord!" Zacchaeus later bragged. "Here and now I give half of my possessions to the poor, and if I have cheated anybody out of anything, I will pay back four times the amount," to which Jesus responds, "Today salvation has come to this house" (Luke 19:8–9).

"So which is right? Give away everything—or just half?" the hot-tubbers wanted to know.

"For Zacchaeus, half was enough. But for this other rich guy Jesus was talking to, it took every penny he owned. That's all we know." That was the guy who believed Jesus was only ever speaking to the person standing in front of him.

Some of the class had heard it preached that Jerusalem had a gate called the "Eye of the Needle," so named because it was too low for a camel to enter without first being unloaded and then crawling on its knees. Others disputed this story as "unbiblical," a word thrown around a lot during quarrels.

Everyone agreed, though, that the new story emphasized not the amount of wealth to be given up but wealth in general as an impediment to faith. I reflected silently—as I'm sure my classmates did as well—that I was glad *I* wasn't rich.

My husband and I were in the process of building a new house because our old one wasn't big enough for our girls to have separate rooms, and I thought about that. *You couldn't really call having a house big enough for your family "great wealth," could you?* I pondered.

After the rich man sadly leaves, Jesus commends those who give up "home or wife or brothers or sisters or parents or children for the sake of the kingdom of God" and promises that they will "receive many times as much in this age, and in the age to come eternal life" (Luke 18:29–30). *Homes*, I thought. *Spouses.*

Children! My two young daughters. My wealth. I could think of no "many times as much in this age" that could replace the loss of the amazing wealth I already enjoyed.

To solve the story of the rich man, my class studied it in all three of its permutations in the Gospels. In one, Jesus augments the commandments he lists in the other accounts—honor your parents; don't murder, steal, commit adultery, or give false testimony—with a more comprehensive commandment: "love your neighbor as yourself" (Matthew 19:19).

Nevertheless, the rich man rashly assures Jesus, "All these I have kept. . . . What do I still lack?" (Matthew 19:20).

Here the accounts diverge meaningfully. In Mark's account, Jesus "looked at him and loved him" (10:21), whereas in Matthew's account Jesus seems a bit incredulous, prefacing his advice that the man give everything he has to the poor with "If you want to be perfect . . ." (19:21).

The Sunday school class leaders honed in on this conditional clause coupled with Jesus' culminating comment, in all three Gospels, that such perfection is impossible for humans but that, with God, all things are possible. That, our class leaders said, was the story's message. God does it all. Not us.

But I fixated on the word *hard*. It is *hard* for the rich to get to heaven. Hard, indeed, for anyone, as Jesus afterward emphasizes to his disciples: "Children, how hard it is to enter the kingdom of God!" (Mark 10:24).

"Why does he say it's 'hard,'" I ventured, "when elsewhere he says all we have to do is believe in him? And, if God really does do it all, then why does Jesus tell the guy to give anything away at all? Doesn't that mean something *is* expected of us—something impossible, like giving away everything we own—but that we don't need to worry about whatever it is because God will empower us to do it?"

My classmates looked at me with their usual mixture of encouragement and perplexity. *What is she not getting?* I heard them wondering.

"I mean, isn't Jesus saying God will simply pull believers' wealth out from under them?"

I envisioned losing our new house, the hardwood floors and expensive windows we'd given up ceiling height to afford. Or losing Kris, the only really nice guy I'd ever been with. Or Charlotte and Lulu, in their little Sunday outfits. A grim scheme. *Such a sacrifice might be* possible *with God,* I reflected, *but that didn't mean it would be pleasant. Certainly not desirable.*

Meanwhile, the discussion surged onward toward 10:45 A.M., when the children's classes would let out and I would need to find some hidden place to nurse Lulu.

"We've already given our farm to God," the group leaders blithely assured us all in parting. I didn't know what that meant, exactly, but I was ready to "give" God our house and daughters if doing so would ensure that God wouldn't just seize them.

Still, I left class feeling we'd missed something in the story of the rich man. Since then, having not only come to faith but to belief in this God who made and loved us and suffered pain on our behalf and wanted us with him badly enough to make it easy, so easy, for us to get there, I have come to believe that what my class and I missed is this: However ardently we might believe, however clearly we might see Jesus before us, however plainly we might hear and understand his promises of rest and ease and release from obligation, we are just like that eager young man. We want salvation to be something we can achieve. We're eager to achieve it. But simultaneously we know we can't. So, like the rich guy, we go away sad.

I think our simultaneous desire and incapacity to do what God is offering to do *for* us is why many of us are unhappy in this life, despite our faith. Jesus offers many recommendations to those who want to save themselves and can't, and the Bible in its en-

tirety offers even more. But for those of us who long for contentment, for the easing of our burdens that Jesus not only
promises but models for us again and again, he has only one recommendation: that we let God do it for us.

4

A Little-Studied Message of Much of Scripture

*The righteous eat to their hearts' content,
but the stomach of the wicked goes hungry.*

PROVERBS 13:25

A SIZEABLE PORTION OF THE BOOK OF LEVITICUS—the bulk of two chapters—is devoted to rules about mildew. It was one of a priest's many mundane tasks to examine people's mildewed items and decide whether they should be washed, dried and kept, or pronounced unclean and destroyed. The writer of Leviticus takes pains to detail what the priest must do in every imaginable instance of mildew that might be at issue: mildewed fabric (woolen or linen, woven or knitted); mildewed leather goods; mildewed houses (stone, wood or plaster); mildew on one side of an object but not on the other; mildews of different colors (reddish or greenish). Each case warranted a different protocol involving everything from examining, washing and drying to scraping off affected parts to burning or discarding the whole item to disassembling it and dumping the pieces "into an unclean place outside the town" (Leviticus 14:40 and 14:41).

This exhaustive itemization of circumstances and responses puts me in the mind of the laundry instructions I composed for my daughters when they went to live on their own for the first time. Separate the clothes into light and dark, delicate and sturdy, and select water temperatures to suit. Examine the clothes and scrub out any stains before you wash: cold water and Mexican laundry soap for protein-based stains such as blood and chocolate, hot water and regular liquid detergent for anything oily, non-Clorox bleach for vegetable-based stains like ketchup and that brown grasshopper spit that gets on clothes when you dry them outside in late summer. Hang up nice clothes rather than dry them in the dryer—it's better for the clothes and the environment—as well as for anything you don't want to shrink, such as your skintight jeans. If you dry clothes in the dryer, fold them immediately, or else you'll have to iron them. And so on.

The instruction regarding mildew in Leviticus is sometimes practical, like my laundry instructions, but other times decidedly religious-sounding. After a mildewed house has been cleansed and replastered and shows no further evidence of mildew, for example, the priest is instructed to

> take two birds and some cedar wood, scarlet yarn and hyssop. He shall kill one of the birds over fresh water in a clay pot. Then he is to take the cedar wood, the hyssop, the scarlet yarn and the live bird, dip them into the blood of the dead bird and the fresh water, and sprinkle the house seven times. He shall purify the house with the bird's blood, the fresh water, the live bird, the cedar wood, the hyssop and the scarlet yarn. Then he is to release the live bird in the open fields outside the town. In this way he will make atonement for the house, and it will be clean. (Leviticus 14:49–53)

The sacrificial requirements for atonement—indeed, that mildew must be atoned for at all—suggests that, when one's belongings get moldy, sin is at issue and that obedience to the mildew rules thus has spiritual value. And in some sense this is probably the case. Certainly, following every last statute, decree, command, and law of Scripture would be a way of showing that God reigns even in the most minor and intimate activities of one's life. It would be absurd, though, to think that God demanded obedience in the matter of mildew as a demonstration of faith or love for him. Rather, God intended the instruction on mildew to demonstrate his own love for us. Mildew poses a danger to one's property and person, and God wanted to protect his children from that danger.

If you have ever spent time in a subtropical environment, you know what a problem mildew can be. When I lived in Hong Kong, I had to put a special heater in my closet throughout the hot summer to keep my clothes from rotting. After Hurricane Katrina, whole neighborhoods of New Orleans had to be torn down and rebuilt because of black mold, which can be a serious health risk. Even here in eastern Oklahoma—which, though not subtropical, nevertheless gets quite humid in the summertime—friends of mine had to abandon their house for good after a flooding rain drenched the carpets while they were on vacation. The whole house was so infested with mildew that it was too smelly to stand and they and their children were perpetually sick.

Although medical research has only recently confirmed mildew as a likely cause of chronic sinus infections and asthma, the writer of Leviticus seems to have had foreknowledge of a connection between mildew and illness. The mildew passages are interspliced with instruction on other seemingly related matters of "uncleanness" like rashes and boils and other diseases of the skin, and mildew and illness are emphatically linked in the summary of these passages that the writer offers before moving on to bodily discharges:

These are the regulations for any defiling skin disease, for a
sore, for defiling molds in fabric or in a house, and for a
swelling, a rash or a shiny spot, to determine when something is clean or unclean.

These are the regulations for defiling skin diseases and
defiling molds. (Leviticus 14:54–57)

In commanding prompt and thorough treatment of household
mildew, God was not seeking to burden his children with arcane
requirements but to protect them from unpleasantness, loss of
property, and disease.

The same principle holds for Scripture's more important rules,
those governing our relationships with God and one another.
Thou shalt not worship statues or anyone else but the One Who
Made You. Thou shalt not kill or steal or work all the time or cheat
on your spouse or neglect your elderly parents. Thou shalt not
covet what the neighbors have or exaggerate what jerks they are.
And so on. These injunctions are designed not only to protect the
potential victims of our malicious selfishness—our spouses and
children and parents and neighbors—but also to keep us, in the
end, from hating ourselves, self-hate being synonymous with depression. To say it another way, mean people live unhappy lives,
and God wants to protect us from that eventuality.

The promise that righteousness leads to happiness—along with
its flip-side, that unrighteousness leads to unhappiness—surfaces
again and again in the Old Testament, especially in the so-called
wisdom literature. In Proverbs we're told that "Whoever seeks
good finds favor" (11:27), "A generous person will prosper;
whoever refreshes others will be refreshed" (11:25), "The desire of
the righteous ends only in good" (11:23), and "those who trust in
the LORD will prosper" (28:25). Indeed, a central promise of the
Old Testament is this: "The fear of the LORD"—that's biblical
shorthand for obedience—"leads to life; then one rests content,

untouched by trouble" (Proverbs 19:23). And while the New Testament may redefine "life" as our heavenly existence, the basic truth housed in the Law still obtains: God's rules are designed to keep us healthy, safe, and happy.

If you're like me, your Bible is full of marginal scribblings and scraps of paper noting exciting insights. Later, when you rediscover what you have written, you recognize your handwriting and may even vaguely remember writing it, but you have lost the passage's original significance, its distinctiveness or urgency among the many passages of Scripture you have taken to heart in your spiritual history, and the scrawled revelation has little meaning for you. A friend of mine once referred to this phenomenon as spiritual amnesia: the loss of a spiritual discovery you once cherished.

My friend ought to come up with a word for spiritual amnesia's opposite: the occasional electrifying moment of recall—often surpassing in excitement the original revelation—when you regain that lost discovery. Somehow, the intervening years burnish the idea with special wisdom and import. To be twice surprised, twice thrilled, by the same turn of phrase or sacred construct is to realize that somewhere deep within you the Spirit of God has been scheming. Positioning the jottings of a lifetime. Waiting for the right moment to reveal and re-reveal. Getting you ready for what will come next, and next, and next. Growing you.

That, in any case, is what keeps happening to me with the revelation that God gave us rules to ensure our happiness. It seems to me that I have discovered and forgotten and rediscovered this fundamental message of Scripture a thousand times, and the notes throughout my Bible attest to my slow learning. Here it is in simple: God is crazy about us, just as we are about our own children, and every command of Scripture, large and small, is designed to protect us from harm and thus facilitate our contentment.

One thing that makes the concept so hard to remember—so difficult, in fact, to *believe*—is that it contradicts experience. Do those

who "Walk in obedience to all that the LORD [our] God has commanded" actually live long and prosper, as promised in Deuteronomy 5:33 and again and again throughout the Old Testament?
Do the righteous always eat to their hearts' content and the stomachs
of the wicked always go hungry, as Proverbs 13:25 claims?

Indeed, the Bible itself contradicts the promise that obedience
leads to prosperity and longevity every time a voice from the
Psalms or Job or Isaiah or Jeremiah or Matthew wails forth a
complaint that the opposite is happening. All around us the un-
righteous prosper and outlive the righteous. Not only that, but the
Bible is replete with stories of people exalted for their faith who
suffer pitiably, and Jesus himself warns believers to expect to
suffer for their faith.

It is easy to explain such contradictions away with the reminder
that no one actually *is* successfully obedient to God's commands.
"There is no one righteous, not even one," as Paul so grimly points
out in Romans 3:10, echoing similar observations in Ecclesiastes
and Psalms.

Still, the key to reconciling the promises of our Father Yahweh
with the bitter reality of his children's suffering lies in understanding scriptural promises as *de*scriptive rather than *pre*-
scriptive. With every rule of Scripture, God hopes to stave off our
misery and generate our contentment by giving us little previews
of the likely outcomes of certain behaviors. The right behaviors
proposed in Scripture don't ensure contentment in every instance,
but, taken as a whole, they up one's chances for health, safety, and
survival—key elements of worldly success and happiness.

The rules of Scripture—everything from mildew regulations to
the mandate that we love the foreigners among us—can be read as
blueprints for contentment right now, in this life, rather than as a
means of ensuring our place in the next. Viewing the scriptural
commands as beneficial instruction in how to be happy rather than
as spiritual tasks significantly reduces the burden of fulfilling them.

5

The Limits of Godly Work

Six days do your work, but on the seventh day do not work,
so that your ox and your donkey may rest, and so that the
slave born in your household and the foreigner
living among you may be refreshed.

EXODUS 23:12

AS A LIFELONG TEACHER IN DIVERSE pedagogical settings—universities, public schools, colleges abroad—I have become a grudging supporter of outcomes-based teaching and the measurable learning objective: that is, a specific learning or behavioral goal with built-in limits that make it easier to determine whether or not the task has been accomplished. I say "grudging" because writing measurable learning objectives is much more difficult than generally stating my goals for a course or an activity, as I used to do. I use learning objectives because, in my experience, they are the only way to set realistic goals for my students and ensure that those who wish to can achieve them.

Take the goal of teaching first grade students how to read, for example. A measurable learning objective might be "Students will recognize and pronounce two hundred one-syllable words." In this objective, the goal of reading is limited in a number of ways: the child is expected to learn only *two hundred* words and only *one-syllable* words, not every word in the English language. The act of reading is further limited, at this early stage of learning, to mere *recognition* and *pronunciation* of individual words, not comprehension or combined usage or meaningful intonation of whole sentences. Such limits help the teacher teach and students learn more effectively, and both teacher and students can know when the desired learning has occurred.

Now, before your eyes start to glaze over the way people's eyes always do at the measurable objective workshops and conferences I've attended and led over the years, let me first assure you that I'm not going to teach you to write them (which is tricky and time-consuming and sometimes seems an exercise in pedagogical absurdity). I won't even encourage you to use measurable objectives whenever you desire a certain behavior of others—employees, clients, students, daughters and sons, the kids in your Sunday school class—and have routinely become frustrated that, though you've voiced that desire a thousand times, no one ever seems to learn it. These are not my goals here. I merely want to point out that God uses measurable objectives routinely throughout Scripture.

Consider the opening pages of the Bible, in which God creates the world and everything in it, including "seed-bearing plants and trees" (Genesis 1:11) "pleasing to the eye and good for food" (Genesis 2:9). Among them are two special trees: "the tree of life and the tree of the knowledge of good and evil" (Genesis 2:9). Soon afterward, God creates humans and tells them, "I give you every seed-bearing plant on the face of the whole earth and every tree that has fruit with seed in it. They will be yours for food" (Genesis 1:29). With one caveat. Having put the man in the luscious Garden of Eden "to work it and take care of it" (Genesis 2:15), God commands him, "You are free to eat from any tree in the garden; but you must not eat from the tree of the knowledge of good and evil, for when you eat from it you will certainly die" (Genesis 2:16–17).

This is God's first measurable behavioral objective: from every tree *but one* the humans may freely eat. Furthermore, eating from that one forbidden tree will result in a measurable outcome: death. This negative outcome implies its measurable converse: namely, successful fulfillment of the desired behavior—specifically, eating only from the permissible fruits and, in general, obedience—will result in God's originally planned outcome for humans: life, pleasurable work (or, in any case, work unlike the "toil" that humans will later be cursed with when they break God's one commandment in Eden), and continuing access to God's many good and pleasing provisions.

Had the first humans stayed in that particular classroom, Eden, and followed God's one command up to that point, they would have lived forever. The first humans didn't obey, though, and God, with that first commandment, established the format of many more commandments in Scripture designed to reeducate would-be garden-dwellers: a very specific statement of desired behavior measurably limited to make the desired behavior unambiguous, realistic, and thus eminently achievable.

But, as I say, the first humans didn't achieve God's original objective for them. Nor do all students always achieve the best teachers' measurable learning objectives. (Had there been a larger pool of initial learners, though, maybe one of them—like Noah, in a subsequent generation—would have gotten that A.) Nevertheless, the possibility of success is apparent from the start. God's overall plan for humans—that they work and thrive in a naturally irrigated garden full of tasty and beautiful food sources, minus the weeds and droughts that characterize even the richest farmlands of the world today—is stress-free, rendered so by God's clear, simple, quantifiable instructions. Similarly, God makes even humans' post-Fall toil more bearable and achievable through the built-in limit of rest: a day's worth for every six days of work and a year's worth every seventh year and an even more comprehensive rest-year every forty-nine years.

Look closely at God's instructions to the Israelites and you will almost always find built-in limits. Humans were to "be fruitful and multiply"—but not outside of marriage or even within marriage with close relatives or on certain holidays or when the wife was menstruating. Similarly, the Israelites were required to donate to charity regularly, but not all or most of what they had or even that portion left over when their own needs were taken care of but a clearly defined and more manageable 10 percent.

Jesus would later reiterate many of God's measurable objectives and create a few himself. So, though the second greatest commandment is often taught nowadays that we should love everyone in the whole world and put their needs before our own, Jesus does not phrase it that way at all. Rather, he tells us to love specifically our neighbors and to love them not *more* or *better* than but in the same way and to the same degree as we love ourselves.

Limits like these built into the Bible's commands, in addition to making desired behavior more doable and precise, emphasize the essence of the task at hand—love, charity, healthy work—rather than oblige perfection. Not that perfection is undesirable. It's just not possible, given our low human aptitude for holiness. Pursuing the impossible goal of perfection will only stress and frustrate us and lead us into guilt.

Behavioral commands with built-in limits are, paradoxically enough, liberating—just as writing a poem according to a formal rhyme or rhythm scheme can be. While following the stringent requirements of, say, a Shakespearean sonnet—three quatrains followed by a couplet in iambic pentameter rhymed *abab cdcd efef gg*—might seem to make the writing of a poem more arduous, less easy and free than "free verse," experienced poets and even poetry students at all levels report just the opposite. Limits on what one may say give poets a structure to follow, a plan of attack, and make the writing of a poem easier than if they were to use no form at all.

Jesus' discussion of forgiveness is especially revelatory of how Scripture's measurable learning objectives work. When his disciples ask him how often they are to forgive those who sin against them, Jesus uses one of his habitual hyperbolic expressions—not the seven times the disciples propose but "seventy-seven times" (Matthew 18:22)—suggesting that God demands almost limitless forgiveness. However, in Luke's account of the conversation, Jesus clarifies: "If your brother or sister sins against you, rebuke them; and if they repent, forgive them. Even if they sin against you seven times in a day and seven times come back to you saying 'I repent,' you must forgive them" (Luke 17:3–4). Jesus limits the command to forgive in numerous ways: You're to forgive specifically *a brother or sister* who has sinned *against you* and only *if that person comes to you and repents* and even then only *after you have rebuked the person.*

These limits on the requirement that I forgive others' wrongs make the mandate considerably less overwhelming and more achievable. I am required to forgive those I consider brothers or sisters, first of all—perhaps not literally my biological siblings but, arguably, spiritual ones. Even then, I'm not only allowed but encouraged to reprimand them before I forgive them. Finally—and, to my mind, most importantly—I'm required to forgive only if they first come to me saying they're sorry. In my experience, continuing to hold a grudge in the face of a genuine and unprompted apology is almost harder than forgiving.

Many believers, and even many nonbelievers, understand the Christian forgiveness mandate to be Jesus' "not seven times, but

seventy-seven times" hyperbole and seem unaware of the comforting limitations Jesus also laid out, which render the sometimes seemingly impossible task of forgiveness doable. Indeed, by
paying attention not only to the mandate but to its God-given
limitations, we allow God to do the impossible task for us.

Even when we remind ourselves that it is not we who achieve
the impossible goal of holiness but God, though, it's nevertheless
hard to get around God's exacting voice in Scripture, commanding
this and that feat of godliness and plainly desiring perfection of us
all. So, I find the limits built into most of God's commands reassuring. It's a lot more manageable a task to love those I come in
contact with—even enemies—than it would be to love everyone in
the whole world. In fact, I don't know what loving someone I never
met actually means. Even forgiving the murderer of one's daughter
or son—which I find inconceivable whenever I read the dramatic
story of such a forgiveness feat in the news—seems more within
my capabilities, though still unimaginably difficult, after a ca-
thartic rebuke from me and an unsolicited and heartfelt expression
of remorse from the murderer.

The pursuit of holiness is not without effort. Jesus says that his
burden is light. But it's still a burden—so much so that most of us
can remember moments when the holy task before us seemed so
immense, so overwhelmingly hard, that the temptation to disobey
or wiggle out from under it won out, despite our most virtuous
intentions. But, as Paul reminds us, God does not tempt our disobedience beyond what we can bear but, when we are tempted to
give up, "will also provide a way out so that [we] can endure it" (1
Corinthians 10:13). The limits built into the divine behavioral objectives of Scripture are one way God ensures that the burden of
obedience is never too heavy.

6

Invitations to End All Commandments

What a person desires is unfailing love.

COMMANDING SOMEONE TO LOVE NEVER WORKS, in my experience. I tried it again and again when my girls were young. Commands that they "love each other" met with the same success as commands that they apologize or forgive each other. While I could sometimes, with harsh enough threats or enticing enough incentives, squeeze the requisite words out of them, I never succeeded in manufacturing by fiat a loving or even halfway cordial tone of voice or amiable attitude, much less a corresponding fondness within their tough little hearts.

I was even less successful when I demanded that my daughters love *me*—typically my last resort in the aftermath of some unspeakable parental malfeasance, such as forgetting Charlotte's tenth birthday. I had already apologized, repeatedly, tearfully, and offered abundant recompense: permission to get her ears pierced—

three years in advance of the previously pronounced age of adornment—along with fourteen-karat gold studs and everything else she showed interest in that day at the mall. To no avail. Charlotte did come to love me again after that, but it took a long time and there was no way she was going to do so before she was ready. While my daughters are both affectionate toward me much of the time, they are never so on demand.

Indeed, I have never managed to force *anyone* to love me. Not best friends I got on the bad side of in junior high school. Not guys I dated whom I liked more than they liked me. Not colleagues whom I have enraged or who have found me obnoxious for one or the other surely legitimate reason. Genuine love, by its nature, cannot be compelled or coerced. The moment one tries, whatever germ of love might have been present shrinks and dies.

And, lest you think my daughters unusually callous and the others I've wanted to love me simply bad nuts, let me say too that I myself have never managed to love under compulsion. I've tried to force myself to love certain people—even to *like* them—and failed. And no amount of commanding is ever going to make me love some unlovable stranger, like the murderers and despots I read about in the news. And if some similar love-feat more relevant to me were at issue, such as loving someone who had done violence to me or someone I love, being *commanded* to love that person would be the surest way to prod me into all-out hate.

And yet, Scripture's two greatest commandments, according to Jesus, are to love. We're to love God with our entire heart and soul and mind—that is, more than we love anyone or anything else—and we're to love our neighbors as ourselves. On these two commandments to love, Jesus says, hang the thousands of lesser commandments that make up the Bible (Matthew 22:37–40).

I like to think of these two greatest commandments as commandments to end all commandments. That's because—and forgive me, Jesus, for disagreeing with your word choice in this instance—commandments to love are not really "commandments" at all. First off, unlike most other mandates of Scripture—don't murder, don't commit adultery, don't tell false stories about others, don't have sex with a woman who is menstruating, don't mix fibers in fabric, don't eat pork—these two greatest commandments are phrased in positive terms. And what we're commanded to do is something people generally want to do. Thus, the two greatest commandments function less as commands than as invitations from God to reach out and grasp the wonderful treasure that not only God but we ourselves all want more than anything else: love.

Ask your friends and acquaintances what makes them happiest in life, and they'll tell you something like "to love and to be loved back." Or, look at the unhappiest people you know and you are sure to notice some crucial lack or loss of love at the root of it all. Childhood abandonment or rejection. The loss—through death or debilitating illness or adultery—of someone beloved. An overwhelming sense of being unlovable. A self-image so damaged as to prevent one from loving even oneself.

Love is the single prize we all want. To love and be loved are the two universal goals of every person on Earth. We may think we want wealth or fame or some other benefit more than love and we often thwart our own attempts to get and give love, but even the richest and most famous people alive would likely exchange everything they had for the perfect love relationship, one in which they are loved fervently and without reservation by someone whom they love back with the same fervor.

Which is exactly what Jesus proposes in that first commandment to end all commandments: "Love the Lord your God with all your heart and with all your soul and with all your mind" (Matthew 22:37). This is God we're talking about. The One who made us. Our Father.

"God, *your* God, is in love with you," Jesus coaxes, "and the only thing God expects from you in return is that you recognize that love and return it." The greatest command in all of Scripture is our Creator's insistent invitation: *Be mine!*

The second commandment to end all commandments, that we love our neighbors as ourselves, is a bit more challenging. To love another human being is to love someone who, in the best of circumstances, cannot love one back as much or as well as God can. Even in their most important and intimate relationships, humans struggle to love without reservation, without impatience or bitterness, without their selfishness getting in the way. Indeed, though we often expect perfect love from others, no human can love perfectly. No spouse or lover can. No child. Not even a human parent.

I know I have fallen short in all of these love tasks. I've never loved my parents or husband or even the two creatures who emerged from my own body—the flesh of my flesh, as it were—as completely or unreservedly, as perfectly, as God loves me. Worse, though I love them as much as it's possible for me to love anyone, I often fail to act as though I do. In fact, the ones I love best are usually the ones to whom I behave the least lovingly. I am less patient, less polite, less kind with my family than I typically am with strangers. I get enraged at those I love more readily. And I'm slower to forgive their own failures of patience, courtesy, kindness, temper, and love than I am similar failures of my students and coworkers and even strangers.

As for my "neighbors," as Jesus refers to the ones we're to love as ourselves, I have to say I invest especially little in loving them. Living out in the country as I do, my literal neighbors are virtually invisible to me, since I can't see them from my house. I do hear news of some neighbors through my mother-in-law. An elderly neighbor has arthritis so bad she can't walk and often cries during their daily phone call. The drug-addicted son of another neighbor has no place to live. Others my mother-in-law tells me about have cancer, marital struggles, financial difficulties, children who've been in car accidents, every sort of problem imaginable.

I am surrounded by neighbors in need of love, it seems to me. I pass the houses they live in when I jog, and occasionally I notice a curtain move or the blue light of a TV light up a window or a door nudge open to let in a dog, and I think, *I should go over there sometime and see what I can do to help.* But then I tell myself I don't really know them or they have their own families to take care of them or the best help I could give would be to pray for them, and that's about as far as I get toward loving them. In truth, I get so tangled up with my own family and job and worries and problems, it's easy to forget neighbors even exist.

But, as Jesus points out, all of Scripture really does seem to hang upon loving one's neighbors. The second "greatest commandment" he identifies is a quotation from a segment of the Hebrew scriptures in which the Lord gives Moses numerous directives concerning neighbors, including "judge your neighbor fairly" (Leviticus 19:15), don't "defraud or rob your neighbor" (Leviticus 19:13) or "do anything that endangers your neighbor's life" (Leviticus 19:16), "Rebuke your neighbor frankly so you will not share in their guilt" (Leviticus 19:17), and culminating in "Do not seek revenge or bear a grudge against anyone among your people, but love your neighbor as yourself" (Leviticus 19:18).

The first five books of the Bible—the Hebrew Law in its entirety—describe every possible way of *not* loving one's neighbors, failures of neighborly love that necessitate restitution and atonement before "they will be forgiven for any of the things they did that made them guilty" (Leviticus 6:7).

Proverbs offers more directives regarding neighborly love: Don't "plot harm against" (Proverbs 3:29) or badmouth (Proverbs 11:9) neighbors or stir up "conflict in the community" (Proverbs 6:19). Don't deny your neighbors mercy (Proverbs 21:10) or take them "hastily" to court (Proverbs 25:8) or even, my favorite, tell them "Come back tomorrow" (Proverbs 3:28). With our neighbors we're to take special pains to be compassionate, patient, forgiving and

available. The prophets recount episode after episode of neighborly hatred and pronounce God's doom upon it. In Isaiah, pitting
"neighbor against neighbor" is, ironically, often God's punishment
for refusing to love one's neighbor (Isaiah 3:5; 19:2), and I hear in
such frustrated pronouncements my own parental voice, cursing
my daughters: "Well, if you can't be nice, then fine, be miserable!"

The word *neighbor*, in English, comes from the Germanic words
for *nearby* and *dweller:* the ones dwelling nearby. The Greek word
for *neighbor* Jesus uses in this second greatest commandment—
πλησίον (*plēsion*)—likewise derives from the word for *near*—πέλας
(*pelas*)—and its essential meaning is "nearby ones." The Hebrew
word most often translated as *neighbor* in English versions of the
Old Testament—רֵעַ (*rēʿa*)—means friend, intimate, or fellow, but a
breadth of meaning is possible. In widely read English Bibles like
the King James and the New International Version, רֵעַ (*rēʿa*) is occasionally translated as *husband, brother, companion, lover,* and
opponent, depending on the context. Neighbors, in other words,
are those we're closest to, the ones we live among and are likeliest
to clash with, the ones we know best.

When Jesus answers the question, "And who is my neighbor?"
with the story of a Samaritan man who lovingly attends to a Jew,
a Samaritan's traditional enemy, left for dead on the side of the
road, he is clearly implying that neighbors include others than just
those of one's immediate neighborhood or nationality or race. But
I question whether he meant *neighbor* to mean "everyone in
need," as is often preached. Rather, a neighbor is any person you
get near to—that is, anyone you actually encounter.

Consider. The Samaritan's neighborly love is ironically intensified by the fact that two of the beaten man's own fellow coun-
trymen, a rabbi and a Levite no less, previously "came to the place
and saw him" and each "passed by on the other side" of the road
(Luke 10:32). In other words, they each *neared* the beaten man
but crossed the road to avoid him. Given the opportunity of

nearness to offer emergency assistance to a "near one," these two holy men—fellow Jews and Jerusalem dwellers, literal neighbors of the hurt man—get as far away from him as they can. The Samaritan, by contrast, considers anyone he nears on his journey—fellow Samaritans or foreigners, the people next door or total strangers, his spouse, children, siblings, even his worst opponent—to be his neighbor. Loving one's neighbor, Jesus is saying, means loving whomever we come upon. Anyone we draw near to in the course of the day is a love prospect.

Loving one's neighbor is, I keep saying, an invitation, not a command. The distinction is perhaps clearer if you've ever lain awake in the night thinking about your opponent of the moment—a person at work, a relative, a friend or loved one you're mad at. Worrying about your conflicts with that person, planning your next attack, your next defense—perhaps, in that moment, hating the person—keeps you from enjoying one of God's greatest gifts to us: deep, restorative sleep.

Indeed, actively hating someone is about as unpleasant and unfulfilling as life gets for me. God invites us, in this second invitation to end all commandments, to put the misery of not loving—and not being loved back—behind us.

Our neighbors are the ones near us. The people we live in the same house with or next door to or down the road from. They are the people we interact and conflict with daily: colleagues, bosses, church members, the checker in the supermarket, strangers we encounter only for a moment and never see again.

Thus, getting near someone can be a transformative opportunity to experience our deepest desire: to love and be loved. So says Jesus' second invitation to end all commandments. Just like the greatest commandment—to return the love of a Father who loves us heart, mind, and soul—the commandment to love others near us is an invitation to enjoy God's most satisfying provision: perfect love.

7

And the Second
Is Like It

Jesus replied: "'Love the Lord your God with all your heart
and with all your soul and with all your mind.' This is
the first and greatest commandment. And the second
is like it: 'Love your neighbor as yourself.'"

MATTHEW 22:37–39

MY ADULT UNDERSTANDING OF GOD—a being at once familiar and enigmatic, lovable and terrifying, who created human beings but also destroyed them—was shaped from the beginning, as I have said, by my own experiences as a maker of human beings. From toddlerhood onward, my daughters frequently seemed to hate each other. They competed, often viciously, for my approval. Just about daily, one daughter would come to me and report some misdeed her sister had committed, demanding that I punish her. When I didn't—being reluctant to punish on demand—I was deemed "unfair." The first daughter would be sullen and the other obnoxiously smug for the rest of the day—or until the smug one came up with an impressive story of sisterly misbehavior of her own to report. And so it went until eventually they took out their enmity on each other more directly and were both punished.

The stories of Cain and Abel, Jacob and Esau, sounded so familiar to me. When I got to the Genesis writer's account of the smarmily holy Joseph—*Hey guys, I dreamed last night you were all bowing down to me!*—and his enraged brothers, I distinctly heard as I read Charlotte's and Lulu's voices, baiting, plotting. Even relatively tame sibling relationships in the Bible—Ruth and Orpah, for example, or Leah and Rachel—acquired, for the knowing parent I was becoming in those days, a grim subtext of bitter rivalry.

Nowhere in Scripture did I see a clearer picture of my daughters' dealings with each other and me—and, by extension, of human beings' dealings with one another and God—than in the story Jesus himself told of a father and his two sons. The younger son, probably enraged at the prospect of inheriting less than his older brother, as would have been the custom, effectively wishes his father dead by demanding his inheritance immediately, before the father had died. When the younger son finally spends every penny and comes home, his sour older brother, not content with the greater portion of their father's estate he still has coming to him, is so resentful that he refuses to take part in the party his father throws in celebration of the brother's return. The father pleads with his older son, to no avail.

"Look!" the son complains. "All these years I've been slaving for you and never disobeyed your orders. Yet you never gave me even a young goat so I could celebrate with my friends. But when this son of yours who has squandered your property with prostitutes comes home, you kill the fattened calf for him!" (Luke 15:29–30).

"Punish him!" I heard the older brother protest in the outraged voice of one of my small daughters. And the story of the prodigal son ends with this convincing picture of the brother's jealousy and rage, while his father tries unsuccessfully to make him understand the nature of a parent's love. I identified mightily with the prodigal dad in the story—with, forgive my impudence, God himself: hopelessly besotted with his contentious children and oddly powerless to make them love each other.

So, I was not only surprised but as pleased with either of my daughters as I have ever been when I read Lulu's response to an essay prompt in her college application process: *Describe an experience you have had, a person who has influenced you, or an obstacle you have overcome. Explain why this is meaningful to you.* Lulu wrote about her older sister Charlotte's being her role model.

In a heartrendingly frank exposé of the despairing envies and rages of sisterhood, she described what it meant to be the second of two same-sex, almost same-age children growing up on a farm pretty much isolated from other kids. From toddlerhood, she and Charlotte were "each other's only and best friends and, at times, archenemies," Lulu wrote. "Being a year older than me, Charlotte could always ride her bike faster, count higher, and dribble a basketball better than I could, and she always made sure I knew it, setting up races and competitions between us that she was sure to win. Inevitably, our play evolved into anger and fights."

Reading Lulu's writing, I suddenly comprehended her history—and, by extension, my own, multiplied by my five siblings—as I never had when it was happening. Her rages. Her abrupt renouncement of any activity—however beloved—in which Charlotte flourished. Her impressive determination, despite a clear desire to outdo her sister in all things, to discover her *own* identity, make her *own* mark, excel in her *own* way.

Had Lulu had more space in her essay—or more sisters and brothers to struggle against—she might have written much more about their childhood antagonism. I know I could have. In Lulu's essay, though—strictly limited in length and written for strangers to whom she probably didn't want to present herself as a budding assassin—my daughters' angers and fights resolved quickly into the deep love they now enjoy. It is a love characterized by shared passions. Solving cryptic crosswords together at Barnes & Noble. *Star Trek*, Ferris Bueller, and the rock band KISS. A silly video game for small children called *Viva Piñata*—involving building gardens to the tune of blithe, hypnotic music—that they still play together today.

As they have matured, their love has grown slowly and raggedly. Though Lulu was proud to point out in her essay that it had survived a three-week teenage road trip, it has also faltered on countless shorter outings—like our yearly Christmas shopping at the mall—and may yet falter or, God forbid, fail. Even outside of the Bible's grim pages, siblings often hate each other, sometimes for a lifetime. My husband and I have, over the years, probably devoted more prayer and worry to the nurturing of our daughters' love for each other than to any other topic of our concern for them besides their faith.

Over the years, we have also devoted considerable financial input to the support of what the girls refer to as "sisterly bonding": movie dates, dinners out, boxed sets of TV series they have fallen in love with at friends' houses (we don't have cable and use our television only for movies), shared KISS paraphernalia. And, although I'm frugal almost to the point of mental illness, this is one expenditure that doesn't bother me. I see it as an investment. From babyhood, my daughters' love for each other is the one thing I have wanted from them more than anything else. And the occasional glimpses I get of their love, as in Lulu's essay, somehow make *me* feel loved.

God, I'm convinced, is the same way. Not only does our meanness toward one another hurt God as no other sin does, but, by extension, our love for one another also pleases God as no other work of holiness does.

Jesus says as much when a legal expert tests him by asking, "Teacher, which is the greatest commandment in the Law?" (Matthew 22:36).

"'Love the Lord your God with all your heart and with all your soul and with all your mind,'" Jesus tells him. "This is the first and greatest commandment" (Matthew 22:37–38).

He could have left it at that and satisfied all present. It was, after all, the Hebrew *shema*, the crux of the Law, which Jews were commanded to teach to their children and bind to their foreheads and write on their door frames and gates and talk about when they sat at home or walked along the road or lay down or got up. Everyone present would have known that answer to the expert's question.

But Jesus went on talking: "And the second is like it: 'Love your neighbor as yourself'" (Matthew 22:39).

And the second is like it. Like it because both are commands to love, one might argue. Or like it in importance, since, as Jesus goes on to point out, "All the Law and the Prophets hang on these two commandments" (Matthew 22:40).

To me, though, what Jesus is saying here is that the two commands are alike. They amount to the same thing. Loving others as ourselves is the best way to go about loving God.

The second commandment also functions as the concrete realization of the first. It is, in other words, Jesus' how-to explanation to the inevitable question of those present who really did want to live out the *shema*: "Yes, but how, exactly, does one go about loving God with all one's heart and soul and mind?"

That, in any case, is how my husband uses the second commandment: as operating instructions for the complex project of living a life pleasing to God. Confronted with a moral dilemma or decision, he doesn't try to read the Almighty's mind. Rather, Kris strives for the most God-honoring solution by applying the Golden Rule. Using his own heart, mind, and soul as meters, he considers the other people involved and sets out to love them as he would want to be loved.

Loving God is not as clear-cut as it sounds, it seems to me. And the holiest intentions often don't make one's path sure, as I learned early on in my adult faith, when I overheard the pastor and elders in my church debating whether to keep on paying rent for a serially jobless alcoholic they'd been supporting for years. Some wanted to continue, while others worried they were contributing to the man's inability to take care of himself by rescuing him over and over again.

"What would Jesus do?" one of them asked—rather sanctimoniously, it seemed to me—and they all nodded sagely.

Then another of them asked, "Well, what *would* Jesus do?" and everyone was of a different opinion. And so the holy debate continued, more hotly than before.

Loving an invisible, inaudible, intangible being like God can be a vague sort of undertaking—often merely a vacant ritual or cerebral exercise—without a plan for how to go about it. Jesus' equation of loving God with loving others as ourselves provides simple, clear direction on how to go about the business of being a Christian.

8

Free Indeed

To the Jews who had believed him, Jesus said,
"If you hold to my teaching, you are really my disciples.
Then you will know the truth, and the truth will set you free."

They answered him, "We are Abraham's descendants
and have never been slaves of anyone.
How can you say that we shall be set free?"

Jesus replied, "Very truly I tell you, everyone who sins
is a slave to sin. Now a slave has no permanent place
in the family, but a son belongs to it forever.
So if the Son sets you free, you will be free indeed."

JOHN 8:31–36

ASK A CHRISTIAN WHAT "A CHRISTIAN" IS, and he or she will probably say a Christian is someone who believes the gospel. Ask what "the gospel" is, and he or she will likely define it along the lines of what Paul calls the gospel in 1 Corinthians 15:3–4: "that Christ died for our sins according to the Scriptures, that he was buried, that he was raised on the third day according to the Scriptures." The gospel, for most believers, is Jesus' sacrificial death on their account.

And this definition is accurate. The crux of the Christian faith is that Jesus died to free inescapably sinful believers from the eternal consequences of their sin.

Consider, though, the word *gospel*, which means simply "good news." As a brand-new believer, I was perplexed that the story of the death of the One God Sent was called "*good* news." News it certainly was in Jesus' day and milieu, and news it still is, centuries later, to anyone who hasn't already heard it. But *good*? How often is the news of the death, much less the torture and murder, of a beloved person considered good? Even if we profited from the person's death somehow—if the person, say, shielded us from a bullet or left us a lot of money—to regard that person's death as good news would be tantamount to hating the person.

Interestingly, though, Jesus' death and resurrection are by no means the only "good news" offered in what we call the "good news"—that is, the four Gospels which collectively tell the story of Jesus' life. The very first "good news" mentioned in the narrative of Jesus' life is the angel Gabriel's announcement of "good news that will cause great joy" (Luke 2:10): the coming of the promised One God Sent in the first place.

Later in his life, this same One God Sent will routinely preach another gospel: the "good news" of the kingdom of God, which biblical scholars and theologians interpret diversely to mean everything from eternity and heaven to a spiritual state of holiness available to believers now. For me, the good news of the kingdom of God is not only the promise of heaven and eternal life but the existence of divine alternatives to what's wrong with our world. Along these lines, Mark characterizes Jesus' message as, simply, "the good news of God" and offers this example of that gospel from Jesus himself: "The time has come," he said. "The kingdom of God has come near. Repent and believe the good news!" (Mark 1:14–15). Elsewhere in the Gospels, the One God Sent preaches the "good news" to the poor, sick, and imprisoned: that their suffering will end.

Jesus himself uses the word *gospel* right before the end of his earthly life in defense of a woman who pours a bottle of expensive perfume on him and rubs it in with her hair: "She has done a beautiful thing to me. . . . When she poured this perfume on my body, she did it to prepare me for burial. Truly I tell you, wherever this gospel is preached throughout the world, what she has done will also be told, in memory of her" (Matthew 26:10, 12–13). Even though, grammatically speaking, "burial" might be understood as the antecedent of "this gospel," Jesus is surely assuming that believers will preach throughout the world not merely his death but his whole story: his coming to our world, his instruction and miracles while here, his resurrection, and his promised return someday to launch our own eternal existence—as, in fact, those who wrote what we now call the "good news" did.

A Christian, I would argue, is one who believes all of these gospels. The gospel of Jesus' birth. The gospel of his death and resurrection. The gospel of heaven, of eternity, of an end to suffering. The gospel of the very existence of our fond-hearted God, who sent someone to us to achieve all these ends on our behalf. Even the gospel of a woman who did a beautiful (though embarrassingly sensual and arguably wasteful) thing: namely, believing in the One God Sent and then acting on that belief in the best way she knew how.

The beautiful thing that woman did would be told whenever the good news of the One God Sent was told, Jesus said, and, indeed, a version of her story is recorded in each of the Gospels. Her beautiful—and idiosyncratic and misunderstood—act represents every beautiful act believers will subsequently perform in response to their faith in the One God Sent.

In other words, what we are called to *do* as believers—how, precisely, we are to live out our faith—is not merely to mechanically follow an impossible list of commandments but something infinitely more personal and real. Some honest expression of our faith in and feelings toward God. And, as in the case of this woman's act—or of David's half-naked street dance that so upset his wife Michal—the ways we choose to express our faith might not conform to others' notions of holiness.

So, to return to where I started out, the crux of the Christian faith is that Jesus died to free inescapably sinful believers from the consequences of their sin. And, as Jesus points out to his followers, "If you hold to my teaching, you are really my disciples. Then you will know the truth, and the truth will set you free" (John 8:31–32). To live the Christian life—in other words, to be a disciple of the One God Sent—is to "hold to" Jesus' teaching, know the truth, and thereby be set free.

Which is a paradox at best, since to "hold to" (or, in other translations, to *stay*, *remain*, or *continue in*) connotes self-discipline and restraint, both of which are antonyms of freedom. In holding to a teaching, we do not allow ourselves freedom to explore alternatives. And, indeed, many believers in the good news view the road before them as anything but free.

Consider. Most believers would agree that what makes them Christians is not something *they* do or don't do but *God's* gracious acceptance of the death of the One God Sent to pay for their failures and sins. They are saying, in other words, that belief in the One God Sent frees them from having to live the perfect life. Many of these same believers will nevertheless keep on trying to live the perfect life and will be secretly disappointed, again and again, when they fail. They don't view themselves as *literally* free, in any ordinary sense of the word. Certainly not free to do what they want. And not free to fail.

Indeed, many believers, when it comes right down to it, do not *feel* free at all. Certainly they do not regard themselves as free to commit the more serious sins mentioned in Scripture: murder, theft, idol worship, coveting, bearing false witness. Many don't feel free to have sex outside of marriage or to abort an inconvenient baby, although they may do these things. Some don't consider themselves free to drink alcohol or marry a nonbeliever or attend an R-rated movie or cut their hair.

And the limits on believers' perceived freedom are not all prohibitions. Many believers feel obliged to *do* certain behaviors, such as go to church or tithe or read Scripture. They don't regard their Sundays as "free" time. Their income is not "free" to spend at will. Even reading what God has to say to us is, for many, not a delight they are free to enjoy but something they *should* be doing instead of reading the paper or checking their e-mail when they first get up in the morning.

Don't misunderstand me here. I'm not questioning the value of any of these common Christian attitudes and practices but rather trying to get at what exactly the One God Sent means about our being "free indeed" (John 8:36). Bible annotators are quick to explain that he's talking about "spiritual freedom"—whatever that means—rather than the ordinary bodily sort of freedom we generally think of when we use that word. Calvin's *Geneva Bible* clarifies in its marginal notes that this freedom is "From the slavery of sin." John Wesley similarly commentates that believers are "free— From guilt, sin, misery, Satan." And the *People's New Testament* explicates Jesus' words like this: "The Gospel obeyed, frees—frees from the yoke of Satan, from spiritual task-masters, from fear, fills the soul with hope and the free spirit of a son who serves the Father from love."

We are, in other words, free to serve God out of love, not obligation. I have tried to explain that sort of freedom to my daughters, arguing that they should serve our family or help me with some task out of love, and they automatically interpret my request as a chore—that is, as an unfair and despised limit on their freedom.

But what if, despite these Bible commentators' clarifications, the freedom Jesus promises steadfast believers was not an opportunity to serve out of love or as a release from sinful behavior but something more akin to what we generally think of as freedom? Not freedom to do what would harm us—as sin always does—but genuine freedom from the physical and emotional stress of striving to be perfect or good or even just adequate in God's eyes. Freedom from the guilt of failing. Freedom from our own pitifully shortsighted preconceptions of what it means to be free at all.

What if our Christian freedom was just what we think when we think of freedom: release from restrictions, the liberty to act as we see fit, liberation from others' authority? What if our Christian freedom was, as the word *freedom* is defined in my *American Heritage Dictionary*, "exemption from unpleasant or onerous conditions"?

What if, in other words, our being "free indeed" was synonymous with enjoyment? Then, surely, we would view God's work differently. We would have no stress, no striving, no guilt. Being a Christian would no longer be a chore or an assignment but an opportunity to enjoy God on a daily basis. It would be pure pleasure.

That woman who went out and spent way too much money on worthless perfume to pour on the head of the One God Sent and rubbed it onto his feet with her hair enjoyed just that sort of freedom. She didn't dither about that act of faith. She didn't worry whether it was enough or whether she was doing it right or whether it was the right thing to do in the first place. She didn't worry about her unworthiness to perform this beautiful act or about what the theologians in the room would say about what she did (which is exactly what they did say). She just believed the good news of the One God Sent and, holding fast to every word, responded.

PART 2

What Ease
Might Look Like

9

Choosing What Is Better

"Martha, Martha," the Lord answered,
"you are worried and upset about many things, but
few things are needed—or indeed only one."

LUKE 10:41–42

ABOUT ONCE A SEMESTER, ONE OF MY STUDENTS has an emotional, relational, educational and—though the student hotly denies it if I say so—*spiritual* breakdown.

Typically, although not always, the student is a woman, but that may just be because I'm a woman, so female students are likelier to confide in me. Invariably, the student was doing well in my course before the breakdown. Better than well, actually. Typically, the woman was a star student: acing papers and tests, asking good questions in class, sending me e-mails to clarify exactly what I'm after in each assignment, organizing study groups and editing sessions.

Always the student is an extraordinarily "good Christian" too. Unlike many of her peers, she follows the university's recommendation that students attend a "home church" on Sunday in addition to the required biweekly chapel services on campus. She's an active member of this home church, often teaching a Sunday school class for younger women and participating in college student Bible studies, mission trips, and mentorships with older women. Frequently, she's a spiritual mentor herself, often to troubled women in her dorm, where she's often the resident assistant or serves in some other leadership role.

It's obvious why she's having a breakdown. She's doing too much. From a spiritual point of view, though, it's not how *much* she's doing. It's *what* she's doing. She's doing the wrong work.

That's what Jesus told his friend Martha, in any case, when she complained about her workload compared to her sister Mary's. All Mary did, as Martha saw it, was laze around "at the Lord's feet listening to what he said" (Luke 10:39).

"Lord," Martha wailed, "don't you care that my sister has left me to do the work by myself? Tell her to help me!" (Luke 10:40).

Jesus could have told Martha that she was doing too much. That's how I usually begin when a good student shows up in tears, two papers behind, certain she's already failed, about to spend the weekend doing mission work in the inner city somewhere, and predictably in the throes of a visceral relational struggle with someone she loves which has activated powerful, destructive emotions. Toxic emissions of stress-anger—annoyance, frustration, resentment, bitterness—brew in some hidden place beneath her holy exertions. Jesus could have offered Martha a tissue and talked soothingly, as I do, about healthy prioritization and life goals. He could have explained this breakdown was her body telling her that she needed to cut back or take time off.

But he didn't. He told her that her stress and the problems it was causing her—the negative emotions, the friction between Mary and her, the fact that she was actually getting little accomplished—was her own stupid fault because she was doing the wrong work.

"Martha, Martha," he clucked, "you are worried and upset about many things, but few things are needed—or indeed only one. Mary has chosen what is better, and it will not be taken away from her" (Luke 10:41–42).

The story ends there. Like most accounts of Jesus' interactions with others, the story is frustratingly elusive. The Bible's not a novel, after all, in which such scenes would be fleshed out. I always find myself wondering, as my daughters always ask at the end of one of my own elliptical dinner table stories, "And then what happened?"

Stories are difficult to learn from. Some say Jesus preached using stories in order to make his messages more readily accessible to simple fishermen and the other uneducated people among whom he lived. I disagree. Certainly the Gospel stories don't support this view. Jesus' disciples are forever asking him to explain his stories and other indirect rhetorical strategies and just tell them what they're supposed to do.

And the Gospels' stories of Jesus' own interactions with those around him are equally ambiguous. Even today, after two millennia of scriptural scholarship, different denominations still prioritize this or that episode in Jesus' life on earth—his washing his followers' feet, his comment that they should remember him when they ate bread and drank wine, his establishment of a church hierarchy with just one of them at the helm—but nobody seems to be on the same page about what these and other stories in the Gospels are telling us to *do* in our daily faith-lives.

For modern readers, the stories in the Gospels—the parables that Jesus told as well as the stories others told of Jesus' life—are additionally insulated against easy elucidation by the cultural differences between the people in the stories and ourselves. We don't have to file divorce papers to get unbetrothed anymore, as Joseph planned to do when he discovered Mary was pregnant. We no longer wear sandals and walk everywhere on dirt roads and thus have to wash our feet whenever we enter a building. We never anoint anyone with perfume or lay out our dead ourselves. Because of such cultural differences, it's tempting to misperceive the *people* of the Bible as different from us as well: holier than we could ever be, more accepting of Jesus' message, less confused about what he meant, probably more obedient than we are.

If we can get past our misperceptions to see the Bible's characters as people just like us, though, it's easy enough to imagine how Martha might have responded to Jesus' remark that her lazy sister had "chosen what is better." She probably rolled her eyes. That's what I'd expect, anyway, from someone who was complaining about her workload to an honored houseguest. Then, I'm guessing, not in the least chastened by Jesus' words or even slowed down in her anger, she let him have it, along with everyone else present—and, above all, her sister at his feet.

"So then, the dinner for all these people is going to cook itself? And the beds will make themselves? And tomorrow's the Sabbath, remember? No cooking, no cleaning, no fetching water? Somebody's got to be prepared for that!" I envision her going on in this vein for a while before stomping out—I'm positive Martha was a stomper and an eye-roller—to get these holy do-nothings' fish and bread and wine on the table and then start in on the preparations for the Day of Rest.

I've heard Martha's words—mostly in kinder, tireder, more resigned voices—in every church I've ever attended. *Somebody's* got to buy doughnuts and get the coffee and lemonade ready for the fellowship hour. *Somebody's* got to write the bulletins and print them up. *Somebody* needs to buy and send flowers for Edith's mom's funeral. *Somebody* has to run Vacation Bible School and make the snacks and drive the bus on the trip to the pool. *Somebody* has to teach the elementary kids' Sunday school classes and run children's church (two somebodies nowadays, if one of the somebodies is male). *Somebody* has to reach the unreached peoples. We can't *all* just sit in the pews, or at Jesus' feet, and do nothing.

That's all we're told about the "better" thing Mary had chosen: She "sat at the Lord's feet listening to what he said" (Luke 10:39). She didn't "do" anything. There were surely many jobs to be done, but, Jesus tells Martha, "only one" was needed: just to sit at his feet and listen.

As attractive as this teaching is, believers routinely resist it. One reason is that just sitting and listening doesn't *look* like work, as we normally understand it. Thus, it makes us worry we "aren't doing enough." It also gets us into trouble with any Marthas around who want us to do our share.

So, unless you're uncommonly good at saying "no"—and the college-aged women who break down in my office are particularly bad at it, in my experience—you'll probably be inclined to take on more work than you should in many areas of your life. And church-related work will be the hardest of all to say "no" to because, after all, wanting to do God's work is part of why we're at church to begin with.

Most believers—even many who know their salvation is dependent on, as Martin Luther exulted, *allein der Glaube*, faith alone!—develop their own private job descriptions for going about the business of pleasing God. These become apparent whenever a believer deems certain behaviors "Christian" or "unChristian." The underlying argument of such labels is that *being* a Christian means *doing* (or *not doing*) x, y or z. Inexperienced believers— particularly excited new members but also our churchgoing children—and even longtime churchgoers are vulnerable to such reassuring definitions.

In Martin Luther's 1552 "Introduction" to his translation of Paul's letter to the Romans, he tries to get at why this is so. "Faith is not what some people think it is," he writes. Believers may observe, for example, that faith—neither others' nor their own—

doesn't always result in "good works or a better life." So they tell themselves, "Faith is not enough" and conclude that "You must do good works . . . to be saved."

What people don't understand, Luther says, is that "faith is God's work in us . . . a living, creative, active and powerful thing" that "doesn't stop to ask if good works ought to be done, but before anyone asks . . . already has done them." Good works pour forth effortlessly from those who believe, Luther says. He is adamant about this. "Anyone who does not do good works in this manner is an unbeliever," he rails, and then he explains exactly what he means by "in this manner": "Faith is a living, bold trust in God's grace" that "makes you happy, joyful and bold in your relationship to God and all creatures."* True faith in the One God Sent, in other words, presupposes God's favor. And, Luther argues, joyful good works result from it.

But the Gospels offer no other details of Mary's good works than that she "sat at Jesus' feet and listened to his words." Although Jesus provides many pictures of what a believer's good works might look like—giving away everything you have, for example, or giving away half of everything you have or putting a hard-won penny in the offering plate—in the story of Martha and Mary he makes it clear that such actions secure neither our eternal salvation nor our present happiness. God neither expects nor even desires us to do more than sit before the One God Sent and listen.

I want to be clear here. In contrast to Luther, who insists that "Anyone who does not do good works" joyfully is not a true believer, I don't question Martha's faith. In the story of Lazarus's death, both distraught sisters reproach Jesus in identical words: "Lord, if you had been here, my brother would not have died" (John 11:21, 32). Jesus responds to Mary by weeping, but to

---

*Martin Luther, "An Introduction to St. Paul's Letter to the Romans," trans. Robert E. Smith (1854; Project Wittenberg, 1994), www.iclnet.org/pub/resources/text/wittenberg/luther/luther-faith.txt.

Martha he says, "I am the resurrection and the life" (John 11:25), and he asks if she believes that. Her reply is one of the clearest, boldest professions of faith in all of Scripture: "Yes, Lord," she tells him, "I believe that you are the Messiah, the Son of God, who is to come into the world" (John 11:27).

Martha indisputably believed in the One God Sent. But she made life unnecessarily hard for herself. Driven by the notion that her exertions were necessary to her own and probably others' salvation, she denied herself the boldly joyful relationship God wants to have with each of us.

The trait that best typifies the students who break down in my office is their great unhappiness. They are believers. Of this I am sure. Certainly they are more diligent believers than I am, to judge from all the good things they are constantly doing. But they are miserable, every one of them. Though they usually manage to get back on track—at least for the duration of my course—I nevertheless sense their continuing resistance to the lesson of their experience in their strained faces in class and careful attention to the smallest detail of my assignments. In their spiritual work-lives, I suspect, they have not changed much either. And it breaks my heart.

10

Giving Cheerfully

*Each of you should give what you have decided
in your heart to give, not reluctantly or under
compulsion, for God loves a cheerful giver.*

2 Corinthians 9:7

EARLY ON IN MY MARRIAGE, I DISCOVERED I had taken up with a man who not only routinely donated money to Greenpeace, the Sierra Club, Amnesty International, Habitat for Humanity, our local NPR station, and every university he'd ever attended but also intended to devote 10 percent of our combined income to charity. Needless to say, we fought about it.

Having lived perforce on next to nothing throughout college and graduate school and my subsequent ten years abroad, I never developed much of a habit of charity. In marriage I enjoyed material resources I had not known since my suburban childhood—a car (and a pickup), a rent-free house, dishes and furniture (some of which matched), and a then-to-fore unimaginable wealth of pretty pasture dotted with cows.

But we were still by no means wealthy. Like other small farms, ours barely earned us enough money to repair our hay machinery and carry us through the months when we had no livestock to sell. Having married rather late, we hoped to start a family right away and settled down in the house of Kris's bachelordom, replete with glass-and-PVC-pipe shelving and a powder blue carpet trodden gray at the front door. His parents had built the "little house," as we called it, after his dad returned penniless from World War II. It had a 24-foot-by-24-foot footprint, with un-insulated plasterboard on the inside and scabby-looking aluminum siding on the outside and a few stones by way of a foundation. Only a splintered pine floor separated us from the dirt—and mice, skunks, bugs, and snakes—below, and nothing but a ceiling fan and a cranky Warm Morning stove kept the humid heat of summer and the winter cold at bay.

According to plan, I became pregnant with our first child soon after we married.

"How can we pay for other people's needs—for whales' needs, for Pete's sake?!—when we can barely take care of our own?" I demanded.

I eventually managed to talk Kris out of Greenpeace, whose questionable politicking was often in the news, and the Sierra Club, with its glossy magazines clearly designed to appeal to rich people nothing like us. And I argued, successfully, that Amnesty and Habitat would benefit more from a donation of our time than from the pittance we could afford to send their way. And when our local radio station reduced its National Public Radio offerings to make room for folksy local programming, I refused to support them anymore. But about supporting his alma maters and especially about that 10 percent tithe, Kris held firm.

As a new member of a church and still relatively unschooled in Scripture, I could hardly find a sound theological foothold for disagreeing, especially when, while studying the history of the early

church in Acts, I happened upon the unsettling story of Ananias
and Sapphira, who were killed on the spot—apparently through
divine intervention—for inadequate tithing. And, though my believing peers disagreed about the details of tithing—whether the
tithe had to be 10 percent, whether it should come from one's net
or gross income, whether nonmonetary giving counted—all agreed
that Christians should donate some regular part of their income to
others in need.

Still, it rankled, especially when cattle prices spiraled downward
and we started talking about my taking courses to become alternatively certified to teach at our local school and Kris's going back to
school as well to study accounting and the seeming riches of the
early days of our marriage began disappearing into an abyss of
fond memory. Every time I saw Kris make out a check to our
church or this or that new charity he was enamored with—Heifer
International, Global Hunger Project, UNICEF—I shuddered,
made a joke about how we were going to have to bed Lulu down in
a drawer of the filing cabinet in our living room, and stewed silently about the leaky water heater and those Sierra Club skiers in
their shiny anoraks and our future.

I gradually came to feel somewhat okay about tithing—which is
to say, I knuckled in to it as my Christian duty. And, in truth,
giving up a tenth of our combined income didn't really affect our
finances discernibly. We weathered the transition from farming to
Kris's new business and my own return to teaching without going
bankrupt. But I still resented the sacrifice.

Then one summer, when the girls were seven or eight years old,
Kris took them to Father-Daughter Camp, where another father
got him all excited about the idea of teaching one's children how to
manage their finances from an early age by giving them money to
dispense with as they saw fit. We're talking an ungodly amount of
money here, in my view—a couple of hundred dollars each, *per
month*. But, Kris stressed to the girls, and to me, out of these funds

they would have to buy not only whatever stuffed animals and electronic gizmos they wanted and the ring pops and candy cigarettes they always begged for in grocery checkout lines but also all their clothes, room décor materials (both were planning bedroom renovations at the time), and presents for friends' birthday parties.

And, Kris told us, the girls would have to tithe 10 percent of that $200—he showed them how to figure out that this would come to $20 per month—to charity. Their choice of charity, but otherwise nonnegotiable.

He explained tithing as a sort of game. They got to choose anyone else's need they found worthy of their monthly twenty dollars—anything from hungry children to missions talked about at church to dolphins trapped in tuna nets. Predictably, they chose charities relevant to their juvenile interests. Guide Dogs of America (they longed to raise one themselves along with our collection of aging farm dogs). The ASPCA. The Arkansas Children's Hospital (Lulu was moved by stories of abandonment in one of their pamphlets). Soon our mailbox was burgeoning with appeals from exciting charities from all over the world: the Center for Elephant Conservation, the Manatee Awareness Society, Tibetan Volunteers for Animals, and countless, equally arcane organizations to help humans.

I piled these pamphlets and envelopes, many of them containing personalized address labels and stamps featuring big-eyed animals and other "free gifts," next to their places at the breakfast table. *Their own junk mail,* I observed to myself sourly. But— though I resisted the $200 allowance from the start and was gratified and appalled to see my worst fears realized as my children evolved into brand-obsessed material girls in their tweens—something about this merry choosing of charities impressed me, and I started taking more of an interest in what Kris and I did with our own 10 percent tithe.

To wit, I started to think of it differently, not as something that was mine that I was reluctant to give away but rather as an increasingly thrilling grab-bag that I got to reach into whenever someone else's troubles touched me. I gave to a luckless janitor at church who needed dental work, an athlete at school who couldn't afford basketball shoes, scholarships at the college where I eventually started teaching, students in dire financial straits.

Kris's accounting business took off and I started making additional money from writing, and soon we had more money to give and, from our expanding contact with those around us, more opportunities to dispense it. Kris did more and more pro bono jobs, which he subtracted from our tithe at his regular hourly rate. Word got around that he did free accounting work for our church and just about any local charity and free tax returns for widows over eighty, and eventually, with both of us thrusting our hands into that grab-bag, we were tithing far in excess of our 10 percent, and we have thus blithely squandered our resources ever since.

Now, I know my thinking on this matter will likely gall those who think one's tithe ought to go to one's church to distribute for legitimate churchly purposes, such as church-sanctioned charities, evangelism, pastor and staff salaries, and church maintenance. After all, churches can't exist without the money members donate to support them, and churches are a wonderful and necessary component of God's intention that not one potential believer miss out on the opportunity to come to faith. In fact—although I have, on several occasions, talked church-tithing friends into diverting their tithe to needed marital or mental health counseling they couldn't otherwise afford—I'm in favor of tithing regularly to one's church if that's the only compelling need that presents itself.

Such rote giving is not my goal in tithing, though. My goal is this: to address a real need I'm specifically aware of and to enjoy doing so in the process. To be, in other words, the sort of giver Paul recommends to the church of Corinth. "Remember this," he tells them emphatically. "Whoever sows sparingly will also reap sparingly, and whoever sows generously will also reap generously. Each of you should give what you have decided in your heart to give, not reluctantly or under compulsion, for God loves a cheerful giver" (2 Corinthians 9:6–7). The result of such cheerful giving—the result, that is, of taking pleasure in tithing—is that doing so enables God to work through us, as Paul goes on to explain: "And God is able to bless you abundantly, so that in all things at all times, having all that you need, you will abound in every good work" (2 Corinthians 9:8). Our very pleasure, in short, is what gets God's work accomplished in abundance.

11

Resting

*Then the man and his wife heard the sound
of the LORD God as he was walking in the garden in the
cool of the day, and they hid from the LORD God
among the trees of the garden.*

GENESIS 3:8

HERE IS A CHALLENGE: DEVOTE ONE DAY per week to genuine rest: that is, to relaxed enjoyment of what you have, rather than working to get more. I don't mean a whole weekend. Just one day. And I don't mean don't do anything at all. Or avoid activities that others consider unrestful.

I mean, rather, do *only* activities you find relaxing and enjoyable. For some, like a childless colleague of mine, teaching Sunday school is an entertainment to look forward to all week. She likes being with children instead of adults and playing games and talking about God instead of all the other topics she talks about during her workweek. Teaching Sunday school is, thus, restful to her, not the frenzied, guilt-fraught burden that it would be for me.

In my case, the most restful day I can think of amounts to getting up a bit later than my usual 5:30 A.M. Reading the latest *Time* magazine for as long as I want while sipping my morning latte. Then sitting out on my porch watching the birds. Then maybe mixing up some flour and sourdough and water and putting it in a greased bowl to rise. Then settling in to a nice long phone conversation with my sister. Digging in my garden. Drinking a glass of wine while I burn a pile of brush. Working on a poem.

You'll notice that some of my restful activities involve exertion. Baking. Digging. Burning brush piles. In my list, I even used the word *work* (though I doubt anyone would categorize working on a poem as actual work). Most of the activities I'm describing here as restful *would* be described as work by some people, though, and are, in fact, activities specifically forbidden on the Sabbath among Sabbatarians—among, that is, devout Jews and Christians who strictly observe the Sabbath.

Don't let yourself be influenced by what others contend are acceptable or unacceptable activities for the Sabbath. Indeed, don't call this day a *Sabbath* at all. That word is far too encumbered by history and controversy to help you get at what I'm talking about here. Call your day, instead, merely a "rest-day."

Give yourself, simply, one full day of rest per week. Let your personal likes and dislikes, your pleasures and stresses, determine what you do or don't do. If *you* find something unrestful—whether it's yard work or cleaning house or washing clothes or getting your family around for church, DON'T DO IT. And if this means your rest-day has to correspond to a different day from your church-day, so be it.

For me, a key unrestful activity is shopping. Whether it's grocery shopping, Christmas shopping, school clothes shopping, even window shopping, it's always wearying. Driving to the place. Looking for a parking place that isn't half a mile away in some creepy-looking outlying lot, then giving up and parking in such a place anyway. Being accosted by people wanting to help me before I'm even all the way in the door of a store. Walking through narrow spaces crowded with choices. Trying things on in weird light. Making decisions. Nothing drains me more than shopping.

Except, maybe, being a tourist. Arriving exhausted from travel in some strange, frantic, tourist-driven city. Wrenching a wadded-looking clean shirt out of a suitcase to go find something to eat. Discovering that, in this place, restaurants close at six in the evening and the street vendors have all gone home to escape people like me and rest themselves. Getting directions to the money-exchange place. Worrying about how much all this is costing.

It is so so hard, in our culture and time, to just rest. Or it is for me, anyway. To get to a still place inside myself where I am aware of how good this life is that I've been given.

When I can get to that restful place, though, I am aware of God as at no other time. The God who created me and everything else in the world and then stopped and rested himself. The God who constantly reclaims me—through the One God Sent, through the words of the Bible, through creation, which testifies continually to God's abiding interest and love.

Though our intentions may be right, in dedicating our pre-scribed Day of Rest to worship and other godly pursuits and even in stringently avoiding what might be considered work, we can miss out entirely on the whole point of God's commandment that we devote one day per week to rest: namely, that we spend time gloriously conscious of God's company.

Consider God's own rest. Often biblical scholars will point out that, etymologically speaking, the Hebrew word for *sabbath* de-rives not from the word for *rest* but from the word for *stop*. The Sabbath, they preach, is about ceasing to work rather than actually resting. Leaving aside the consideration of whether this argument might have its roots in the reality that some believers—such as church staff and those members of the congregation who perform church business—can hardly look forward to a truly restful Sunday and someone has to do all the work that allows church to happen, I want to look a bit at the model of rest presented in Scripture: God's rest, that is, after those six days of creating order out of chaos and creatures to enjoy it and, out of dirt and his own breath, people who resembled him.

Although the Hebrew noun for *Sabbath* first occurs long after the creation story in Scripture, in among the many rules that Moses passes on to the Israelites, Sabbatarians generally take us to the word's verbal root in the model story of God resting in Genesis: "By the seventh day God had finished the work he had been doing; so on the seventh day he rested from all his work. Then God blessed the seventh day and made it holy, because on it he rested from all the work of creating that he had done" (Genesis 2:2–3). God, they say, stopped working, and so should we. And, in some sense, I agree.

Substitute the word *stop* for *rest* in the passage, though, and you will see that there is a problem in this way of thinking about the Sabbath: "By the seventh day God had finished the work he had been doing; so on the seventh day he stopped all his work." Doesn't the fact that God "had finished the work" imply that God has already stopped? If so, then what is the new activity—heralded by the conjunction *so*, suggesting causality—to which the second half of the sentence refers? To what *different* behavior does God turn after stopping work?

I think the answer lies in the comparison of what God does before stopping and what he does afterward. In the verse immediately before God finishes his work, we're told, "God saw all that he had made, and it was very good. And there was evening, and there was morning—the sixth day" and "Thus the heavens and the earth were completed in all their vast array" (Genesis 1:31 and 2:1). God's work is "completed" and "very good," so it makes sense that he stopped working and did something else.

Immediately after we're told that God "rested from all his work," the writer of Genesis focuses our attention on the humans in the garden and retells the creation account from their perspective. The narrative returns to God's post-creation activities only after the man and woman botch the first divine work assignment—to "take care of" and "work" the lovely garden God had made for them (Genesis 2:15), to manage the animals, to make babies, and to abstain from the fruit of a certain tree—and their eyes are opened to their own inadequacy. At that moment, we're told, they "heard the sound of the LORD God as he was walking in the garden in the cool of the day" (Genesis 3:8).

In my view, it is here—ironically in the context of the humans' failure and not in the mere stoppage of God's work—that God models what resting really means. Walking. In the garden. In the cool of the day. Clearly enjoying himself.

Evidently God was making noise as he walked—perhaps merely the crackling of leaves and fallen twigs underfoot, but I always imagine that God was making the sort of noises *I* make in *my* garden, along with all the creatures around me, the birds and the bugs and our dogs, Moe and Erica: we sing and sigh happily and hum and commune with one another, enjoying out loud how wonderful God's creation is and how wonderful it is to be part of it and, by extension, how wonderful God is for making it all. It is this, this conscious enjoyment of God's delightful provision to us, that I call resting.

The psalmist seems to be thinking along the same lines in urging us, in the persona of God, to

"Be still, and know that I am God;
    I will be exalted among the nations,
    I will be exalted in the earth." (Psalm 46:10)

The psalmist's word here, רָפָה (*rāpāh*), though a fairly common

word in the Old Testament, is translated as "still" in most translations only in this one passage. Elsewhere it means to go limp or
slack, to let go or withdraw or give up, to sink, to relax, to be lazy.
Pharaoh uses *rāpāh* pejoratively—twice, to emphasize its negative
value in his eyes—in response to Moses' request that the Israelites
be allowed to hold a three-day party in the wilderness to worship
their God.

"Lazy, that's what you are—lazy!" (Exodus 5:17), Pharaoh tells
them and orders them back to work.

I read God's instruction to "Be still"—Be lazy!—"and know that
I am God" as a simple presentation of cause and effect: that is, if
we would just quit trying to *do* our faith and instead relax and
enjoy the life we've been given, then we would become more in-
tensely aware of God. And, as the psalm continues, our natural
response to such awareness would be exaltation. Continually
working without resting, in other words, blinds us to God's beauty
and goodness and power and, above all, to God's repeated
promises to do all the work for us.

Loving God, in short, naturally develops from allowing ourselves genuine rest—the sort of rest which many might feel guilty
to embrace: the lazy, humble enjoyment of all that God has accomplished on our behalf. Mary, in electing to sit at Jesus' feet
instead of setting the table or washing up after the meal with her
sister Martha, chose this rest.

And Jesus invites us to share the same sort of rest when he
beckons, "Come to me, all you who are weary and burdened, and I
will give you rest" (Matthew 11:28). Like Pharaoh, he then repeats
the key word of his message, *rest*, for emphasis: "Take my yoke
upon you and learn from me, for I am gentle and humble in heart,
and you will find rest for your souls" (Matthew 11:29).

12

Yoked to the One God Sent

Do not plow with an ox and a
donkey yoked together.

DEUTERONOMY 22:10

THE YOKE IS A POWERFUL METAPHOR IN SCRIPTURE, used most often in reference to domination and subjugation. Old Testament writers bewail the yoke of oppression and the yoke of slavery, and the God they write of frequently threatens the yoke of slavery and oppression as punishment for disobedience and promises to break the yokes of those who obey. In the biblical perspective, the yoke is the metaphorical antonym of freedom. And, while Paul counsels "All who are under the yoke of slavery"—that is, actual slaves—to accept their lot and "consider their masters worthy of full respect" (1 Timothy 6:1), he elsewhere declares, "It is for freedom that Christ has set us free. Stand firm, then, and do not let yourselves be burdened again by a yoke of slavery" (Galatians 5:1), by which he means our slavish devotion to evil.

The yoke is also a symbol of uniting efforts with another. The

Law warns against unequal yoking of draft animals (Deuteronomy 22:10)—presumably because the variance in their strength and shoulder heights would make sharing work more difficult—and later the apostle Paul metaphorically echoes this warning in reference to the marriage of believers with unbelievers, who are, according to Paul, as antithetical to each other as virtue and sin, light and darkness, God and idols (2 Corinthians 6:14).

Scriptural yokes are intriguing in any discussion of God's work since the real-world purpose of a yoke in the farming culture of biblical times was to make it possible for two or more draft animals to share the same task, thus rendering the work easier for each of them than it would have been if one were doing the work alone. In other words, the original purpose of a yoke is to spread, or equalize, work, making it possible to get more done while reducing the toil and stress of those involved. This understanding of the word *yoke* is seen in cultures today where water is still carried balanced from a yoke in two manageable buckets rather than lurched along in one unwieldy bucket. Yokes make work easier by dividing a load, and yet, semantically, they suggest anything but ease. The yoke has somehow evolved since biblical times from a means of sharing labor with another and lightening one's load to become the quintessential symbol of enforced labor, the worst kind of work imaginable.

All of which serves as a paradoxical backstory to Jesus' invitation: "Take my yoke upon you and learn from me, for I am gentle and humble in heart, and you will find rest for your souls. For my yoke is easy and my burden is light" (Matthew 11:29–30). The One God Sent is not our taskmaster or subjugator, and the yoke he speaks of is not the yoke of oppression or slavery or even of toil. Indeed, we are invited to take this yoke upon ourselves not for work at all, but for *rest* from work.

The yoke of the One God Sent—metaphorically, the work of God—is thus unlike anything we might normally think of as work.

It is not a burden. It does not make us weary. It does not enslave or oppress us. Rather, it is the antidote to stress and toil: a source of relaxation and pleasure. What God wants of us in the way of work is akin to what we think of when we hang up the "Gone Fishin'" sign on the door: fun, escape from the unpleasantness of our jobs, rest.

I never go fishing, literally speaking, although I love to eat fish and, living on a farm, I am surrounded by ponds full of fish. One reason I don't fish is that I don't have any fishing tools except for an ancient, decaying pole that belonged to Kris's dad, who died long before I met Kris and apparently used it in some faraway time before his crippling rheumatoid arthritis would have made tromping to the ponds more of a trial than an enjoyment. If I wanted to fish, I'd have to go out and buy a new pole and hooks and floaters and sinkers and line and an orange vest so that lurking hunters wouldn't mistake me for a deer and shoot me.

More important than my lack of equipment, though, is that I don't have the fishing habit. In my family, past and current, there's never really been a tradition of fishing that would have given me the know-how and patience and, above all, the *desire* to fish—to wake before daybreak, as some students and friends tell me they do, with the urge to enter the dark, ticky woods in search of catfish or bass or whatever fish swim in our ponds.

My dad did go deep sea fishing a few times in my childhood, on a chartered boat with enormous poles attached to the deck for catching bluefin tuna. He came home with mainly sharks, though, which the real fishermen who manned the boat laughed at him for not throwing back in. And once he took my siblings and me down the road to some unknown neighbor's pond, where we trespassed to catch perch so flat and puny we couldn't even cut them in half to get their bones out before frying them.

Here is that memory: I was maybe nine. We were newly arrived in the Connecticut countryside from suburban southern California. It was hot—a breathless, about-to-storm, East Coast kind of hot unlike what I knew of West Coast hot. On our way to the pond, my siblings and I fought over who got to carry the cheap pole my dad had bought for us all to share and the coffee can full of writhing nightcrawlers we'd caught the night before by shining a flashlight on their coital forms and shocking them into immobility. By the time we arrived at the pond, we were happy to let my dad carry everything. Indeed, my brother, who was just four, begged to be carried himself.

The thick sour air and black raspberry brambles around the pond dike and our dad's long legs compared to our short ones made the mysterious adventure increasingly unpleasant. The pond was shallow and full of muck and had a fishy, musty outdoor smell none of us liked.

First we had to find a clear spot from which to cast, our father told us, so the hook wouldn't catch in the trees overhead or brambles beneath. When we finally found a place he thought would work, we clustered in close to watch him pull a squirming nightcrawler out of the can and murder it on the hook. Then, he stood tall and tossed the hook out over the water, where it snagged in the invisible network of decaying branches below the surface and had to be tugged and cursed back to us, minus its hook. The next try was the same, and the next, but he eventually managed to land the hook in a good place, whereupon he gave my older sister the pole and showed her how to reel it in if she felt the pole move. She stood alert and we all waited. And waited. Finally, my dad took the pole from my sister and reeled in the hook. It was bare.

"Didn't you feel anything?" my dad asked, clearly irked. Sharon shook her head without looking up. Still, my dad conceded, if the worm was gone, there must have been a fish out there to eat it.

We spent the rest of that sweltering afternoon, in my memory, waiting. And scratching ourselves bloody from mosquito bites. And not daring to complain for fear that our dad might do to us what we watched him do over and over to those worms. Eventually one of us, probably my dad, caught the first of several perch, but I can't remember a moment of triumph when a little glinting sprig of life was jerked from the water. My memories of that fishing trip are strangely fishless. And itchy and hot and unpleasant.

So, when elderly relatives of Kris invited us all—Kris, his mom, me, and our toddling daughters—on a trout-fishing trip somewhere in Missouri, I wasn't enthusiastic.

I had some notion of the additional exertions and unpleasantness trout-fishing might entail. In the attic of our Colonial-era house in Connecticut, my sisters and I had discovered a gargantuan pair of waders for fly-fishing that some previous tenant had left there. And much later, as an English major in college, I read Hemingway. I pictured Kris and me wading through rushing streams of icy water, onion sandwiches stinking in our pockets, our daughters flailing on our hips, while Uncle Charlie flicked the hook back and forth over the surface of the water—possibly right in little Charlotte's sweet face as she craned to *see-e-e-e-e-e-e* what he was doing. It seemed even unlikelier we'd catch any trout than when my siblings and I fished for perch from the banks of that pond.

"How are we going to fish for trout with the girls?" I asked my husband.

He shrugged. "They say it's a place where you can take kids."

"But how, 'take kids'? Charlie and Frances never had kids. They have no idea what taking kids means. They're probably thinking they'll park me and Mamaw and Frances and the girls in the woods somewhere while you and Charlie fish. And then, after the girls are good and cranky and haven't had their naps and are covered with bug bites, we can have a picnic of warm tuna sandwiches and drive three hours back home."

Kris shrugged again. The relatives were insistent. And, though Kris does not have the habit of fishing, he does have the habit of complying with elderly relatives' wishes. So we went.

It turned out there were no woods, no ticks, no wading, no fly-fishing even. Although the mountain-fed stream was icy cold with the clear water I guessed trout needed to thrive, the portion of the stream devoted to this family-friendly trout hole was too deep to wade through and screened off on in both directions to make catching a big one possible even for toddlers like Charlotte and Lulu. The trout literally leapt from the water for the canned corn the farm owners pressed into the girls' baby hands. Although Charlie did help Charlotte hold a pole and pull forth what he taught her to call "a whopper"—that trout was a good foot long!—the main way the girls "fished" was with a net: Kris or I would put one girl's little hands on the long handle and then, holding her by the waist with one arm, helped her scoop up trout after trout. Both girls were wholly pleased with themselves and with the fish they caught, and they had such a grand time and worked so hard they fell asleep as soon as we got in the car to leave and slept the whole way home.

Something like that job of fishing is what the One God Sent is talking about in inviting us to collaborate with him and find rest, I think. If ever there were an unequal yoking, it is this: we put our hands on the handle of the net and aim for the glint in the water at our feet, while the One God Sent grasps us around the waist and, taking firm hold of the handle along with us, pulls a heavy, squirming fish into the sunlight. In carrying out the work of God, the exertion is all God's. Our only input is the pleasure, the excitement, and the willingness to be there in the first place. And we sleep sweetly all the way home.

13

Loving Siblings and Other Family Members

*Then Jacob prayed, "O God of my father Abraham,
God of my father Isaac, LORD, you who said to me, 'Go back to
your country and your relatives, and I will make you prosper,'
I am unworthy of all the kindness and faithfulness you have
shown your servant. I had only my staff when I crossed
this Jordan, but now I have become two camps. Save
me, I pray, from the hand of my brother Esau,
for I am afraid he will come and attack me,
and also the mothers with their children."*

GENESIS 32:9–11

I FEAR I MAY BE PRESENTING GOD'S WORK as requiring no effort whatsoever from us, so I want to reiterate that this is not so. Doing God's work entails the often daunting effort of acting on one's trust in the promises of the One God Sent regarding work: that, however impossible it may seem, it will be easy and will result in pleasant rest. God's work is not a matter of just gritting one's teeth and obeying the call to act, though, but convincing oneself that the job will result in restful ease. And convincing oneself to accept God's promises—that is, believing that all things really are possible with God—takes effort, especially if the task before you comes with a history of impossibility.

Consider Jacob's wrecked relationship with his twin brother, Esau. The two were enemies from birth—nay, according to Scripture, from before birth. They fought in their mother's womb. Their rancor was intensified by Esau's advantages—which Jacob surely regarded as unfair—as the just barely firstborn of the two. As a teenager, in any case, Jacob tricked Esau out of not only his birthright but their dying father's blessing. Having sown so much discord in his already dysfunctional family, Jacob then got as far away from them as he could in the subsequent years. Then, God told him to go home.

The relationship between the two brothers seems doomed beyond repair, and Jacob is legitimately terrified of Esau on the eve of their eventual reencounter as adults. Yet, in Jacob's prayer before the encounter with his brother, he focuses on God's promise that his obedience will result not in the violence Jacob fears but in prosperity. And, miraculously, so it does. In one of the most surprising and heart-warming moments in Scripture, the brothers reconcile.

With this story in mind, I want to consider familial love. In presenting loving one's enemies as more difficult than loving one's "own people" (Matthew 5:47), Jesus seems to suggest that loving one's own family is effortless and automatic. And often this is so. But often our own people don't love us. And, even if they do, they're nevertheless the ones we're likeliest to conflict with and thus the hardest to love back.

Story upon story in the Old Testament confirms the difficulty of loving one's family—particularly siblings. Think Cain and Abel, Joseph and his murderous brothers, Mary and Martha, the prodigal son and his angry big brother. Clearly, family members who ought to love one another effortlessly often don't.

As an accountant, my husband interacts daily with families struggling over matters of money, so I regularly hear accounts of siblings hating one another, parents and children not talking, spouses maligning each other to their children, people hating their parents-in-law, families divided along emotional front-lines as dangerous as war zones. The Bible is full of stories of just such families.

In fact, if we're unloving or uncivil toward anyone in our lives, it's likeliest to be family members, those who should be easiest to love. And it's in these crucial lifelong relationships that we can do the most lasting damage. More than any mission work to distant strangers, our most important love legacy to the world might well be our spouses and children, our parents, our siblings and their children, because it is through these familial relationships that we create others capable—or incapable—of loving others.

Perhaps that's why Jesus so often speaks in terms of siblings when he talks about love. He calls his followers his brothers and sisters and says of those in need, "Whatever you did for one of the least of these brothers and sisters of mine, you did for me" (Matthew 25:40). Reconciling with one's siblings takes prece-dence, Jesus says, over other offerings to God: "First go and be reconciled to them; then come and offer your gift" (Matthew 5:24).

He says being "angry with a brother or sister"—and who, with siblings, has not been?—will be punished as harshly as murder and that siblings who call each other names are "in danger of the fire of hell" (Matthew 5:22). But, again, what sibling has not called another sibling "Stupid-head!" or spoken maliciously about him or her to others? What angry girl has not pinched or scratched her sister? What older brother has not lorded it over the younger? What younger brother has not sought revenge? Worse than all these, what member of a large family has not nurtured bitter or uncharitable or unforgiving thoughts about a brother or sister long since estranged—that is, made a stranger?

Loving our neighbors as ourselves begins, I think, with the ones who were near to us from birth: our siblings and other family members. And not just the ones we're currently "close to" but the ones we should be close to but are fighting with or aren't talking to or can't stand to be around. The ones toward whom we feel bitter or fed up or unrelated by choice. The ones who have become our de facto enemies.

But how, oh how, does one make the task of loving these ones not merely effortless but pleasant? That was my prayer some years ago with regard to my own distant close ones.

I come from a big family of strong personalities. We are loud and opinionated and combative, each difficult in his or her own way. Although as children my siblings and I shared parents and experiences and clothes and beds, we were never very "close to" one another. Then, when our ages ranged from early adolescence to early twenties, tragedy drove us even further apart. Our mother became, as we thought, mentally ill and then was operated on for a brain tumor. Her resulting disability and eventual death and the host of relationship-destructive coping strategies that often accompany such family tragedies—rage, blame, drug use, depression, flight—scattered us far from one another for good, it seemed, relationally as well as geographically.

My own habit of dealing with pain in those days—absenting myself from it—drove me more out of contact with my siblings and parents than anyone else. I moved ever farther from our southern California home: New Orleans, Boston, Berlin, Beijing, Hong Kong. It seemed to me I couldn't get far enough away from the ones I grew up "close to," and, although I had no particular hatred for my siblings, they were soon strangers to me. I made occasional visits home before our mom died and then, for many years, no visits at all. I was too busy with my own spouse and children and nearby friends, and my siblings were equally busy with theirs. Only guilt spasms occasioned by a Christmas card from one or the other family member—I myself had long since abandoned even that token mode of bonding—motivated me to reconnect with an occasional phone call. Once, one of my siblings-in-law vied to acquaint our kids with one another. But we were already too distant, I felt, to rebuild—or build anew—any kind of closeness. So, to my shame, I rebuffed those efforts.

Some years ago, inspired by that shame and by my siblingless husband's habit of reading Scripture literally, I decided to be more intentional about loving my actual brothers and sisters. Sibling by sibling, I am lurching my awkward way back into closeness with my family, and I have this to report about the pleasures gained: My sisters and brothers are a sweet, sweet discovery I wish I'd made earlier in life. Though we remain physically remote from one another, our shared history of nearness really does connect us in unexpected ways. Often I find them speaking my thoughts or revealing to me truths about our past that I would never have discerned on my own.

As for the exertion involved, my only hurdles have been prompting myself to call on a schedule and then finding time to talk on the phone. I solved both problems when I came up with the idea of calling one or the other sibling during my long slow runs on the dirt roads near my house. Our conversations make the time pass quickly—certainly a boon—and I exercise thereby not only my leg and abdominal muscles but my heart muscle as well, in all of its dimensions: physical, spiritual, emotional, relational. Running has become, for me, love training, and, like all true love, it is its own reward.

Once, on a long run that had become too long when I realized I had neglected to make a turn and was lost, I tried to get my sister Dorothy on the phone and ended up chatting for five miles with my nephew Mark, a loveable young man in his twenties whom I had met only once, when what would become his personality was still encased in the mute shyness of boy-adolescence. We talked about his friends, his worries about one of them, their custom of occupying empty lots to play football. Who knew that adults, that anyone, played pickup football games? What kind of person would have enough acquaintances to assemble two opposing teams? We talked on about these mysteries as I sweated and panted, about his generation's networking skills and about connectedness, his and mine. Mark—formerly a name, a guilt at Christmastime, another unrelated relative—became a person to me on that run, and, for a moment or two of that conversation, I think I became a person to him.

Long after I had already arrived home, I was reluctant to hang up. I lingered in my driveway talking to him as if he were an old friend, as if he were family.

14

Getting to Remorse

*"When he came to his senses, he said, 'How many of
my father's hired servants have food to spare, and here
I am starving to death! I will set out and go back to my father
and say to him: Father, I have sinned against heaven and
against you. I am no longer worthy to be called your
son; make me like one of your hired servants.'
So he got up and went to his father.*

*"But while he was still a long way off, his father saw
him and was filled with compassion for him; he ran to his
son, threw his arms around him and kissed him."*

LUKE 15:17–20

ANOTHER DIFFICULT LOVE TASK, FOR ME, is repentance. Most
times, when I do something wrong, I am typically blind to my own
error. Even in those rare cases when I can't avoid noticing it, I am
reluctant to acknowledge my fault to the one I have wronged.

It pains me to divulge that my daughters entered this world

entirely incapable of remorse. When, as toddlers, one would hurt the other one, even by accident, I had to force her to say she was sorry.

"If you trip over the cow pens your sister has spent the past hour building out of LEGOs and Tinker Toys and blocks, the nicest and least dangerous response is 'I'm sorry. I didn't mean to do it.' At the very least, you should say, 'Oops!'"

The resulting apologies were hardly expressions of true remorse but merely hollow exercises in cordiality, like the thanks-absent "Thank you" I extracted from them in response to a treat or a kindness.

"If someone gives you a lollipop," I taught them, "you say 'Thank you.' Unless, of course, that someone is a male stranger and Mama is out of sight. In that case you scream and run . . ."

I made them go through the motions of these exchanges, again and again, without much evidence or even expectation of true gratitude or remorse.

And there was none. Whenever they got into fights, each was sure her sister was entirely in the wrong. Once I had extracted the requisite expression of guilt and left the room, they took up the matter of blame with teeth and nails. When they eventually made up, it was always a relief to me, but if the making up involved not merely the passage of time, as was usually the case, but one or both of them expressing sincere repentance and being forgiven by the other, I felt the deepest possible love for them.

When they got older, they took their conflicts out into the world of friends, teachers, coaches, and teammates, and, increasingly, me and my husband. There, corporeal resolution gradually evolved into the combination of diplomacy, avoidance, and anger repression we often refer to as "forgiveness." But getting to a meaningful "I'm sorry" remained a rarity. Whenever it happened, though, the moment I sensed that the child might be even on the verge of acknowledging partial culpability for a wrong, I was flooded as at no other time with an intense sense of my daughters' goodness and lovability.

My daughters' accomplishments I treasure most have not been their winning of spelling bees and scholarships or even their occasional room cleanings or (regrettably few) offers to help me in some unappealing task. Rather, I cherish the even rarer occasions on which they have expressed remorse—to me or each other or anyone else.

Our heavenly Parent is no different, judging from the countless calls to repentance in Scripture. Throughout Scripture, God suffers because of our cruelty to one another, so he presumably enjoys our occasional repentance and attempts at reconciliation. I imagine God's greatest parental pleasure is when we recognize and regret our meanness and express sorrow for it—to one another and to him. Not surprisingly, Jesus' first preaching on "the good news of God" was a call to penitence: "The kingdom of God has come near. Repent and believe the good news!" (Mark 1:14–15).

The giving and receiving of remorse are learned skills. Nevertheless, aside from that routine demand for an unmeant apology extracted from us in childhood, if we are taught anything at all about remorse—by our parents, in our churches, at school—it is that we should forgive others' misdeeds (whether or not they express remorse, many will even stipulate), not that we should learn to feel or express remorse ourselves when we do others wrong. No one ever trained *me*, in any case, in how to initiate reconciliation in a conflict. And only a few courageous friends ever recommended that I strain my eyes past my own blinding self-righteousness to search out my own fault in a conflict. So, when I consider myself wronged, I typically believe that I am entirely in the right and the other person is entirely in the wrong.

Case in point. Once, in the early days of my faith, when I was determined to do the right thing if it killed me, I got into a fight with a fellow teacher about a room we shared. I was new at the school, and my classroom was the computer lab, where I taught writing to tiny classes of struggling seventh graders. Upon being hired, I learned it was my responsibility, in addition to teaching my classes, to look after the computers, turn them on in the morning and off when not in use, and see to it that no one abused them. My colleague, a veteran teacher, had been taking his much older students to the lab for years, and he clearly resented my class's and my presence in the lab from the start.

"We have nowhere else to go," I told him and suggested he and I switch rooms for the duration of his class, but he said that wasn't a possibility: Only high school students were allowed in the high school building, where his classroom was. Had I been around longer, I might have offered him plenty of examples of exceptions to this rule. Indeed, I could have proven to my satisfaction, if not his, that there was no such rule at all. But I had only been teaching there about a month and knew little about how things worked at the school. So, my little class and I stayed in the room, and my interaction with my colleague became ever more caustic. Soon, we were talking almost not at all and weaving wide paths around each other as we moved among our students.

This was back in the early days of personal computers, and the lab was prone to paralyzing failures. Sometimes the computers— quirky little Macintoshes with everything but the keyboard all in one little box together—overheated and just quit. Or the kids, de-spite my best efforts to keep tabs on the lab during my lunch duty, would sneak in and mess with the passwords, somehow overriding my administrator's password such that I could no longer open anything. Once, a group of seventh grade boys got in and trans-formed the beep noises the computers made whenever you back-spaced into fart noises and curse words.

Locking the door didn't seem to make any difference. Countless people had keys, and the principal said there was no money for new locks. So, I started turning off all the computers right before leaving for lunch. My thinking was that, as long as it took for the computers to reboot, the kids wouldn't have time for much chicanery before I was back in the lab.

As luck would have it, my colleague's class was right after lunch. Although I always got there early so the computers were only seconds away from being ready to use by the time our students were in their seats and heads had been counted, this new source of friction—especially that I had unilaterally put a solution into practice without consulting him—rubbed our antagonism into a full-out fight. He yelled at me as at a child, right in front of my students and his, and I went home that day angrier than I'd ever been at someone not related to me.

Coincidentally, I had been reading about anger in Scripture, hoping to convince my husband that anger was not sinful—Jesus got angry, after all—and that stuffing anger, as Kris was in the habit of doing, was unhealthy and futile. That very morning, however, I'd read a scary passage from one of Jesus' sermons that was making me rethink my views:

> "You have heard that it was said to the people long ago, 'You shall not murder, and anyone who murders will be subject to judgment.' But I tell you that anyone who is angry with a brother or sister will be subject to judgment. Again, anyone who says to a brother or sister, 'Raca,' is answerable to the court. And anyone who says, 'You fool!' will be in danger of the fire of hell." (Matthew 5:21–22)

Anger, it seemed, was tantamount to murder and made one in peril of hellfire.

Of course, I hadn't called my colleague a fool, but I certainly thought he was one. In truth, I thought him worse than a fool, and I called him *that* when I recounted the story to my husband that evening. Still, I detected the unmistakable trail of the Holy Spirit through the whole matter, and, although I knew that this man was entirely at fault, I also knew what I had to do.

The next morning, I got to school early and went to the man's classroom. I've never been a noticer of who drives what car, but somehow I knew as soon as I got to the parking lot that the lone car there was his. I sensed, in fact, that he was a hardworking, good teacher, in his way, and not the bad word he had become in my mind.

The smile he had for the student or colleague he assumed would be opening his classroom door vanished when he looked up from his gradebook and saw me, and it took every ounce of who I am to force myself to express convincing remorse. I lied that I should have shared authority over the lab with him, should have consulted him before making changes that would affect his teaching. If I had it to do over again, I told him—if I had our entire acquaintance to do over again—I would have operated so differently.

The curious thing was, as soon as these words left my mouth, I actually felt them to be true. I suddenly saw, as in a vision, all the little ways I had been intentionally combative toward this man. In truth, I confessed to my most inner self—who knows such things anyway but likes confessions—that I'd felt as intruded upon by this man and his snooty high-schoolers as he must have felt by me and my ridiculous seventh-graders. Our distrust and hatred was mutual, our culpability in the conflict about equal.

My apology tipped the balance, though. Expressions of remorse tend to disarm an opponent, I have since learned. In any case, we forgave each other, on some level, immediately. We even hugged.

In our subsequent interaction, we gave each other plenty of opportunities to practice not only forgiveness but remorse. I became, as I like to call it, his main forgiveness project, and he mine. What a blessed relief it was not to hate him anymore!

Some part of me—that wise inner self, perhaps—learned from this experience that shared culpability is at issue in most conflicts, so I look now for my own blameworthy actions and attitudes whenever I feel wronged and have become many people's forgiveness project since those days. Every new time I offer myself in this way, I think of my girls and how I feel when they reconcile after a fight, and I know that God is thrilled.

15

Looking After Widows and Orphans and Other Needy Neighbors

Religion that God our Father accepts as pure and faultless is this: to look after orphans and widows in their distress and to keep oneself from being polluted by the world.

JAMES 1:27

VISIT A NURSING HOME OR A SCHOOL and you will discover that, as in biblical times, the elderly and the children of broken homes are among the most neglected and vulnerable and needy people in our world. Statistics will bear out your observations, but perhaps the most persuasive testimony will be your recognition of, in another's words or expression, an unmistakable hunger for company and attention. For the kindhearted among us, recognizing that hunger may be enough to cause them to visit—or at least to feel enough guilt for not doing so to take some other sort of useful action. But for hard-hearted ones like me, it takes a bit more.

Thus it was that, as my elderly, widowed mother-in-law gradually quit doing the few activities she still engaged in after her retirement from teaching—quit gardening, quit driving, quit having enough going on in her life to carry on an interesting conversation—I stopped having much to do with her. Eventually, it would become apparent to my husband and me that her retreat from the world was the beginning of a slow, creeping dementia. Even in those early years, though—long before she lost the ability to form an opinion, follow a conversation, read a book, or understand the weather report on TV—being around her was increasingly a chore I dreaded, something I knew I *should* do rather than something I *wanted* to do.

"She repeats everything she says," I complained to Kris.

"She can't talk about anything but what she and the girls did during the day."

"If she doesn't stop interrupting what people say at the dinner table to offer them food they can get for themselves, I'm going to strangle her."

This was the woman who had looked after my toddling daughters when I went back to work—who, in her seventies then, climbed trees with them and helped them dig potatoes and cut okra in her garden and taught them both to read and write long before they ever entered school. She lived only a quarter of a mile away, on our farm, so we saw her daily. Many times daily, since, when she wasn't overseeing the girls, she was zealous to feed us and help us vaccinate our cattle or separate the weaned heifers from the steers or generally help us out in any way she could. Whatever she had was ours, and this was a resource we dipped into repeatedly, especially early in our marriage, when we were still trying to make farming work. We used *her* riding mower, *her* tiller, *her* pruning shears, and we borrowed money from her to buy more land and replace farm implements.

Scriptural injunctions to look after widows aside, Mamaw—as

the whole family referred to her from the time the girls were little—was every bit entitled to my company and my love. I owed her that much and more. But, after the girls started school and quickly grew up and away from us, all I had to offer this kind, selfless old woman was duty, barely masked annoyance, and secret prayers of shame that I wasn't able to be more loving.

"I do not understand what I do," I wailed inwardly, in the words of Paul. "For what I want to do I do not do, but what I hate I do" (Romans 7:15).

But repentance and even envisioning myself in the same circumstances forty or fifty years hence—slow, self-obsessed, repeating the same feeble question over and over again, the same worry about where the girls were and what they were doing—didn't seem to change my attitude. So it was that Mamaw became my New Year's resolution every January. My albatross. The main source of guilt in my prayers.

My publishing career was beginning in those years, and I reduced my teaching to accommodate my new job of writing, revising, sending manuscripts off for approval, then getting them back and revising a second and often a third or fourth time.

I worked in the quiet of my otherwise empty house, the only way the composing part of writing can happen for me: with the girls at school and Kris at work and no noise or activity to interrupt my train of ideas. Even then, the empty house distracted me, and I often wasted the morning cleaning bathrooms, doing laundry, making bread, planning a meal for the evening, and generally giving in to the household and its demands. I forced myself to visit Mamaw daily, as soon as I got the morning chores accomplished, and always returned home so cranky with her and mad at myself I could hardly concentrate on anything else. Above all, I was peeved that I only had an hour or two to work before the girls got home and I wouldn't be able to try to write again until the next day.

So it went until I finally managed to get a draft on the page.

After that came revision, which didn't require isolation. Indeed, quite the opposite.

"The best way to revise," I'm always telling my writing students, "is to read what you have written to someone else. Out loud. Not to the empty air but to a warm, listening body. Not, mind you, because any feedback from the other person, beyond laughing at the funny parts or looking bored, is likely to help you much. Rather, you need to hear your voice addressing a real person and trying to get your point across. Only then can you hear what isn't working or what sounds unnatural, what you need to twist and rearrange and re-see to make it better."

I don't remember how I first got with the idea of reading my writing aloud to Mamaw—whether I came up with it or God intervened in response to my groans. It's hard to find someone willing to sit through the reading of even a short chapter, much less a whole book. Kris was tired when he came home from work, and my girls were too young to be interested. Mamaw may simply have been a last resort.

In any case, I started reading my essays and chapters aloud to her, highlighting errors as I read and redundancies and phrases that sounded awkward. I could tell from the expression on her face when her attention was flagging and knew then that I needed to cut. Eventually, I read her each of my first three books in their entirety at least twice through.

Mamaw loved it. She felt so honored that I had chosen *her* as my primary audience and critic that she bragged about it to the occasional friend or relative who called. She made a show of checking if she had her hearing aids on when I got there and insisted on making a pot of her horrible coffee before we started and pouring half of it into the big red cup that she had decided was my favorite. Once I started reading, though, she never interrupted or glanced away or fidgeted. And when I finished reading the selected piece for the day, she always offered the same uplifting assessment:

"I think this is the *best thing* you've ever written!" I could see from her face that she really meant it. And even though she repeated those same words each time and they could hardly have been true, nevertheless I loved hearing them. My reading times with Mamaw were sheer pleasure for both of us.

Mamaw's infirmities have progressed to the point where our shared reading sessions would be too much for her, and I have to look for pleasure in her company in other ways. Lately, it's cooking together, another love of mine that is now a struggle for her. Instead of cooking food and taking it down to her, I raid her freezer and cupboards for the makings of a pot of beans or the red vegetable soup she used to make that was my daughters' favorite food when they were little.

I plop an ancient pound of hamburger meat—still good, I decide, since it's bright red and I found it at the very bottom of the coffin-like freezer out in her utility room—into her biggest stockpot and then have Mamaw open cans of green beans, corn, and tomatoes with the new easy-to-use can opener I bought her, while I chop up onions and potatoes and whatever other vegetables I can find in her refrigerator drawers. Then, in tandem, we dump these ingredients into the boiling pot and wait for it to come back to a boil. After a while, I fish out the meat, fork it into chunks, and put it back in.

"You used to tell me you put cumin in," I remind her. So we rummage through the spices in her refrigerator freezer door for a little glass jar of it, dated 1972 yet still as fragrant of sweat and ethnicity as cumin always is. I drop in a tiny pinch and then some salt. Soon, it's ready, and we each eat a bowl of what she says I made and I say she made, and it's good. Then I ride my bike back up the road and get to work on the next chapter.

16

"I'd Rather Do It Myself"

The woman came and knelt
before him. "Lord, help me!" she said.
He replied, "It is not right to take the
children's bread and toss it to the dogs."
"Yes it is, Lord," she said. "Even the dogs eat the
crumbs that fall from their master's table."
Then Jesus said to her, "Woman, you have great faith!
Your request is granted." And her daughter
was healed at that moment.

MATTHEW 15:25–28

I LOVE TEACHING PEOPLE HOW TO WRITE, especially the brand-new college students in my yearly English 101 course.

"No other course is as essential to your academic success," I tell them. "Not math. Not Western Civilization. Not even *Global Civilization*."

Nowhere else will they focus as exclusively on the essentials of academic discourse: generating ideas, supporting them with evidence, using others' opinions to refine one's own. Nowhere else will they practice such fundamental life skills as questioning, struggling to understand, arguing a point, getting others interested in their views. Nowhere else will they receive as much personal attention and feedback on what they say and how they say it. When I teach English 101, I believe I am empowering them not only as future scholars and professionals but as useful citizens, good parents, informed believers: viable participants in the world's doings.

My students don't usually see it that way, though. For most, English 101 is a pointless chore—a hoop to jump through, as I have more than once heard the course described. Students either think they already know how to write and thus have nothing to learn, or else they've always struggled as writers and despair of ever pleasing a teacher well enough to get an A.

Thus, although most universities require first year composition and although most incoming students genuinely need it, they increasingly test out, if they can, or else take some less demanding version while still in high school, unaware that this course, more than any other, will establish their future success.

Consequently, the typical English 101 class comprises a few international students fresh out of English as a Second Language (the ones who'll make the As) and those who either failed the Advanced Placement test or weren't motivated enough to come up with some other way to avoid the required course. My English 101 students, in other words, all struggle as writers and stand to learn much in college composition.

The international students pay attention and take notes, even on the first day of class, when all we're doing is getting acquainted and going over the syllabus. The rest look glum. Every paper they've written since elementary school, they'll report on the writing inventory I've assigned for our next meeting, was returned to them covered in indecipherable criticisms. They sit silent, eyeing my exacting syllabus on the first day of class, certain I'm going to do the same thing.

They're right—I too will scribble inscrutable messages all over their papers—but I go out of my way to dispel their fears. For every assignment I clearly outline exactly what they must do to make an A, and I guarantee them all 100 percent on their first essay.

"You don't have to be a great writer to do well in this course," I promise. "You just have to learn to write better than you currently do, and you do that by showing up and following my simple instructions."

I prophesy the problems they'll have in the course of the semester and offer strategies for dealing with them: "If you can't get a paper done—it just won't come, say, or you used up your writing time having fun—don't skip class and miss the reading quiz. Just hand the paper in late. I only take off 10 percent per class-day late."

The international students write this down.

"Also," I continue, "I cry easily, especially when someone's writing is really good. I can't read Rilke or Dickens aloud without sobbing. Even student writing—sometimes just one really good sentence in an essay full of errors—can make my voice crack. If your essay is so good it makes me tear up as I read, you get an automatic 100 percent, no matter what's wrong with it." (The international students will spend the rest of the semester writing maudlin essays, mistakenly thinking that's what it takes to make me cry.)

"And," I tell them, "I'm available to work with you during my office hours. Not just available. I *want* to." Perverse as it sounds, there are few activities I like better than struggling through a chaotic mess of words with a student, helping him or her figure out what's being said.

"Come go through a draft with me!" I beg. I repeat this invitation many times throughout the semester, often soliciting the international students who take me up on it to stand up and give their testimonies of how it went in my office.

"She helped me know what I'm saying," one woman reports.

"I fix my grammar," says a jolly student. "Get 100 percent on that part at least!" He winks in my direction.

"She made tea," another student says.

"She don't bite me," another student adds.

Few native English speakers take advantage of my standing offer of one-on-one help, though. I hear them silently protesting, as my brother Larry once responded to our dad's offer of help on a project involving an X-Acto knife that ended up almost severing his thumb, "No, thanks. I'd rather to do it *myself!*"

So, toward the end of the semester, when finals are looming and students are stressed and worrying about grades and attendance is lagging because they're busy with papers for not only my course but all their others and most are regretting whatever fun they've had since arriving on campus, I talk to them about work and success and the inevitable trials and traumas of life.

"Let's say it's the end of the semester, and you've got three research papers due the same day."

Several of them nod knowingly.

"That's what we do," I joke. "All your professors get together over coffee and decide which day will be our collective due date. It's our big entertainment every semester."

Edgy laughter.

"But, really, imagine you have these three papers due and then, of course, finals to study for. Then you get news your grandpa is in the hospital and your family's talking like he's going to die. He's your favorite relative—though he probably doesn't know it since you haven't had time to call or write him in, like, forever, 'cause you're so busy."

Nods at the word *busy.*

"Anyway, Grandpa's in the hospital and you can't go see him. Too far away. Too expensive. Heck, let's say he lives in Ecuador," I add, nodding toward a clump of international students from there. Some of them are probably in exactly these circumstances: loaded down with schoolwork, homesick, and preoccupied with the sufferings of a faraway loved one.

"You're so distracted by worry you don't feel like doing any work. But you have to. Your family's paying lots of money for your education, money they don't really have. So you keep at it. But then, as if things weren't bad enough, your computer crashes, and you lose everything and have to start all over."

They all look at me expectantly, thinking a punch line must be coming.

"You've already returned your Interlibrary Loan books. And you didn't keep a record of the articles you used. And that's just for one of your papers. There's no way now to get your papers done. What should you do?" I ask.

Silence.

For once, I allow plenty of time for everyone to figure out that I really mean my question and to consider an answer. It's a question so important that I'll ask it again on the final exam.

Eventually, when the silence gets embarrassing, answers trickle in.

"Time management," someone offers.

"Too late."

"Work harder!" several say at once.

"Not possible. You're already working as hard as you can."

"Quit socializing," someone else says.

"Nope. Even the time you spend socializing—even the time *Matt* (or whoever the class partier is) spends socializing—won't be enough to catch you up."

Silence again for a while.

"Pray," someone ventures.

"Nope," I say. Because I teach at a Christian university and many students are devout, my negative answer shocks them, so I amend it somewhat. "I mean, go ahead and talk to God about your situation. Praying's always good. But is that your whole plan? You're just going to just sit there and wait for God to fix everything? Or is there something you can *do*?"

"But you said there's *nothing* you can do."

"Did I? Well, there is one thing. Only one thing."

Again silence. In all my years of teaching, I've never once had a student offer the correct answer, but I'm always hopeful. It would be so much more powerful coming from one of them.

Finally I have to tell them.

"The one thing you can do is this: Go to your professors, explain your situation, and ask them to cut you some slack."

Once again silence. I can see from their faces this is the last thing most of them would do.

"What's the worst that can happen? They say, 'Tough luck, it's due when it's due.' And the best thing that can happen? They say, as a professor once said to me after such a disaster, 'Forget it. I don't even want to *see* that paper. You're getting an A.'"

Here's the thing. I tell my students again and again that my goal is not to punish them but to help them learn, not to fail them but to ensure their victory. I long to fulfill not only their dim hopes of surviving with a passing grade (and never having to take writing again) but my own much loftier ones: that they learn and grow and become more effective people as a result.

"I'm on your side," I insist throughout the semester, and I take pains to demonstrate it by limiting my expectations to what is entirely doable. Success in my English 101 class is as easy as paying attention.

Nevertheless, though they'd love to please me—that is, get As—most students don't take me up on my offers of making it easier for them. Few seek my help. Ignoring my simple plan for their success laid out in the syllabus, they see only those scribblings in the margins of their papers and convince themselves that only perfection will do. As the semester's end approaches, they toil as never before and come up with extra credit schemes on top of what's due to try to recoup a grade they could have aced if they had merely taken advantage of my routine clemency.

That's how we are with God, I think. God builds rest into our work—mandates it!—and limits most of Scripture's commandments to make them not burdens but almost effortless opportunities to please. Just as I want my students to succeed, God wants *us* to succeed. All we hear, though, are the *Thou shalts* and *Thou shalt nots*. All we can see is the abundant evidence of our failures to please an exacting God.

In faith, we need to be like those international students who get the As: not stressing over the professor's—or their own—expectations of perfection but attentive to the minimum required and boldly taking advantage of every aid held out to them. Every loophole. Every respite. They're in my office wanting help so often that I have to wean them after a couple of drafts to help build their confidence in their own writing ability. I have learned to say *wean* in several languages—Spanish is *destetar*, German is *entwöhnen*, French is *sevrer*, Chinese is *duànnǎi*—to surprise them and make them laugh in that tight moment when I tell them that, on the next draft, they're on their own.

Although they start out at a disadvantage as non-native speakers of English, my international students earn their As—and write better and learn more than their native speaker peers—not by striving harder or stressing out but by shamelessly accepting every crumb of assistance I toss their way. Often, despite my efforts to wean them, they keep on showing up at my office door and in my e-mail in-box, begging for help, sometimes on into the next semester and the next year, when they're not even in my class anymore. And though I rarely give in—indeed, if it's for help in another course, I never do—nevertheless I respect them for trying. That's how I'd like to be in faith: taking seriously all the evidence that God is sincerely committed to my success.

PART 3

Clutching the Curse
of Toil

17

Good Works

*I do not understand what I do. For what I want
to do I do not do, but what I hate I do.*

ROMANS 7:15

WHEN, AFTER A DOZEN YEARS OF ATHEISTIC LONGING, I returned to the Christian beliefs of my youth, I was ready for faith:
starved for the certainties that began to fill me once my sense of
my Creator's realness was reestablished and eager to make up for
my lost years by serving God in everything I did.

Exactly how to go about doing the work of God, though, confused and worried me. The Bible, fellow believers, pastors, and my
own conscience offered endless directives. From the moment my
faith returned to me, I felt surrounded by voices, each one ad-
vising "Do this!" or "Don't do this!" Serving God seemed an impossible task.

My own husband's views on God's work were especially
daunting. He read the Bible daily and took very seriously what he
told me were the only commandments that really mattered: Love
God, and love your neighbor as yourself. He strove to live a life of

obedience to those commands. He devoted himself to our family and his widowed mother and assisted anyone who needed him, especially our literal "neighbors" on the farms surrounding ours. He lent them money, helped them with their taxes, tutored their children. When their cattle escaped or their plans to have their hay baled fell through, we put our own haying and cattle work on hold to help them.

Kris's devotion to others sometimes perplexed me, especially when he put their needs before our own. Nevertheless, as a fervent new believer, I wanted to do God's work too. So, when we became official members of a church and were immediately recruited to lead something called children's church, I readily agreed, even though it meant that I would miss out not just on the normal service and the teaching I was so hungry for, but on the company of others in my circumstances: recently married with small children and jobs, somehow balancing parenting and spousing and jobs with God's work. As a newcomer to the region and the church and even the ways of believing practiced in the region where we lived— so different from the Roman Catholicism of my childhood—I was a stranger in so many ways. I needed to be with fellow adults, not rowdy children slapping their bodies and howling, *"Father Abraham had many sons, and many sons had Father Abraham!"*

Secretly too I yearned for an escape from my own two children, who sang and slapped themselves—and whined and spilled and tussled and seemed to do anything but worship—along with the rest of the kids in children's church. Taking care of Charlotte and Lulu was hard work, just as hard as my other jobs as a teacher and my husband's farmhand. No, harder. One of the main attractions of church for me in those days was a respite—however brief—from the grueling work of managing others' children for most of the schoolday and then coming home to spend the rest of the day and the better part of the night feeding and diapering and entertaining and comforting and cleaning up after and worrying about my own children. I longed for a calm moment. For rest and an opportunity to reflect quietly on God and learn more about my faith. I yearned for the tranquil company of adults who knew more about God than I did.

I'm not ready to teach anyone, I wailed inwardly. *I don't know enough about God myself.*

Still, the church leaders had chosen Kris and me for this ministry, they said, because they saw us with our kids and knew we'd be good at it. And so children's church, which I felt ill-equipped and unmotivated to lead and which stressed me more than any of the other work I did, became my Sunday job.

Kris, it turned out, loved children's church. As an only child and lifelong believer who'd never attended any church, he discovered in it a spiritual camaraderie he'd always coveted: fellow believers to get rowdy and have fun with in honor of the God he loved. Kris is a gifted leader of children and, at another church we attended after getting burnt out at this first one, went on to teach the youngest Sunday school class, a job he plugged happily away at every Sunday, long after our own children were too old even to help out in class.

I, meanwhile, developed an ill-hidden aversion to Sundays. I dreaded getting up early, wrestling the girls into the fancier clothes that I'd be rinsing hot chocolate stains out of when we got home, nudging them into their Sunday school classes, then bustling back down to the moldy basement to set up cookies and drinks and activities for children's church. *What does any of this have to do with God?* I was still wondering two hours later, as I sorted the giant Legos we had donated to the church from the other toys and trash on the floor and put them back into their grimy bin.

Nevertheless, despite children's church, and despite my ongoing effort to do what I believed was what a believer was supposed to do, I still worried I wasn't doing enough to serve God. Visit the imprisoned. Feed the starving. Spread the message of

God's love to someone who'd never heard it. But I had neither time nor energy to do any of this good work.

I am useless at this business of serving God, I decided. *A failure.*

One Sunday afternoon, on my weekly trip to the supermarket, I turned on the radio. There was nothing on NPR, so I surfed the stations till I landed on a booming voice that exactly articulated my disappointment with myself as a worker for God. The man was talking about spreading the gospel.

"What are you waiting for?" he thundered. "The woman at the well didn't wait. She didn't put off doing God's work until she was a mature believer. Or until she had a free moment. She just dropped that water jar and started telling people about God! That's what you need to do. Just get out there and do it!"

I sat in the Price Cutter parking lot and berated myself for a long time before I finally got out of the car and strode into the store. I surged through the aisles looking for someone to help, someone to tell, someone upon whom to work out my salvation with fear and trembling. The store was nearly empty. The few people I encountered were too preoccupied with their shopping to meet my eye. Eventually, I gave up, loaded my cart, and wheeled it up to the register.

In front of me in the line a slight woman was slamming her few groceries—two cans of soup, a box of toaster pastries, a liter of Mountain Dew—onto the belt, huffing loudly to hurry the purchase ahead of her. Tattoos vined her arms. Her skeletal face had a stretched look. When she asked the checker for a carton of cigarettes, though, her soft voice seemed at odds with her hard appearance and angry gestures. She sounded timid, hopeful even, and unbelievably tired. I was certain God had put her in precisely that place at precisely that moment for me to approach and love.

And so, I concentrated all my inner resources—energy, desire, faith, determination—into the task before me and . . . said . . . did . . . finally . . . nothing. The checker, offering the few words that the monetary exchange required, was more successful in chatting the woman into some sense of being cherished by a loving God than I will ever be, and I left the store ashamed and defeated.

Many years would pass before I found confirmed in Scripture the lesson of my own experiences: that, as Paul complains in his letter to the Romans, our holiest exertions will fail. As hard as we try to do otherwise, we will continue to do what we hate to do and not do what we want to do or feel we should. Or, if we succeed in forcing ourselves into some holy work—as I did with children's church—it will not fulfill us.

Helping the less fortunate and educating others about God are certainly work and probably worthy undertakings, and I do not mean to question the value of such efforts on the part of my fellow believers. That said, if we view these or any other spiritual tasks as doing God's work, we are setting ourselves up for lives of stress, failure, and unwarranted guilt.

18

Saying No

*What do people get for all the toil
and anxious striving with which they labor under
the sun? All their days their work is grief and pain;
even at night their minds do not rest.*

ECCLESIASTES 2:22–23

❧

ALTHOUGH CHILDREN'S CHURCH STRESSED and exhausted me on my only designated Day of Rest and made me unenthusiastic about Sundays in general, nothing could have been further from my mind in those days than to quit doing it. I was, I reasoned, now an official member of the church and ought to do my part. So, I passed out the juice and cookies and cleaned up the mess while Kris told the squalling kids Bible stories.

And when my girls got a bit older and school was out for the summer, it never occurred to me to refuse, when asked, to help run the church's summer vacation program called Vacation Bible School, which was children's church magnified into a daylong nightmare that lasted a whole week, with five times as many kids—

the regular kids from church plus scores more from the surrounding neighborhood whose parents had seen the sign on the marquee and wanted a week of relaxation and free childcare.

Nor did I say no to any of the godly duties that I was urged to perform when, a few years later, I took my current teaching position at a Christian university. I helped new students move into the dorms and volunteered at their orientation activities. I assisted older students in various missions, and I met weekly with still others as a spiritual mentor. Steadily, my life of service burgeoned into a frantic source of bitterness that kept me from enjoying the very thing that got me involved in such activities in the first place: my consciousness of God's presence and love.

In short, the more involved in God's work I became, both through our local church and in my church-related job, the more involvement seemed to be expected of me, and the more determined I became to do it all. Thus, before I had acquired even the most basic understanding of my new faith, while the dew of my spiritual awakening was yet upon me, I was already experiencing burnout, though I wasn't really aware of it. I was ever more tired and God seemed ever more distant, but I mistook my frantic activities for faith itself and went after it with teeth-clenching fervor.

I was determined, in fact, to do *more* than what was asked of me. I invented new holy projects for myself, in addition to what was already filling my weekends and free time. I volunteered to lead a discussion hour between services and contributed to the church newsletter. I also offered to write some of the health advice flyers that University Health Services posted in the campus bathroom stalls. We needed to focus, I told the nurse, on spiritual, not just bodily health.

One of these flyers, inspired by a problem I had noticed among the students I mentored and especially those students who ended up in my office on the verge of breakdown, finally revealed to me my own spiritual infirmity. It was entitled "Be Nice and Say No" and began, "Developing the ability to say no is often ignored in the maintenance of physical, emotional, relational, and even spiritual wellness. Often, our very niceness gets in the way of doing the right thing. In the name of niceness or because we don't want to appear unwilling to help others in need, we often find ourselves overcommitted and resentful."

I identified church requests as "particularly difficult" to say no to, and I gave advice out of my own failure on how one might go about saying no in such situations: don't offer any reason for saying no, which just provides the asker with leverage with which to pressure you into giving in, and plan a stock response in advance that will give you time to consider whether you really want and have time to fit whatever it is into your schedule. Have an accountability partner, I counseled, with whom to discuss whether you have time for a new responsibility and whether, in the unlikely event that you do have time, this particular project is worthy of your attention and effort.

I concluded that "Saying no, even though it may seem unkind, is often the healthiest stewardship of your gifts and resources and sometimes the only way to avoid disaster."

I never really got to the crux of the matter, though: Saying no to the burdens others want to load onto you is saying yes to God's real work, which, as Jesus told the stressed-out would-be workers around him, is simply "to believe in the one he has sent" (John 6:29). Our work is to *believe* Jesus when he says that his burden is light and his yoke is easy and that sharing the work with him will not stress or overwhelm us or cause burnout but rather will give us rest (Matthew 11:28–30).

Our very stress, as well as any feelings of guilt we might have that we don't "do enough" as believers, I have come to think, are meters of spiritual health and, as such, instruments of spiritual renewal and growth—much as pain, though unpleasant, serves the positive function of alerting us that something is wrong with our bodies and inspiring us to take it easy and seek healing. It humbles me to admit how often I have had to relearn that nothing whatsoever is required of me beyond believing in the One God Sent. I keep wanting to think otherwise.

To think otherwise, though, is to embrace not God's promises of the richness or contentment or rest that results from healthy spiritual work, not Jesus' assurance that the work itself will be easy, but the curse of the Fall, when the pleasant work of the Garden of Eden was transformed, through our own doing, into hard earth and thorny weeds and toil.

It's tempting to read the curses God announces to the first humans as penalties for misbehavior. I think, though, in light of God's and later Jesus' promises of prosperity and ease, that these curses are, in fact, not so much punishments—and, as such, inescapable realities of this fallen world—as predictions of what we're going to choose for ourselves. Given God's presence, we would choose independence. Given God's gift of companionship, we would choose enmity. Given God's provision, we would choose struggle.

Toil is not our fate, in other words, but our lot. In cursing Adam and Eve, God was telling them, "Henceforth you will see even the pleasurable work assignments I offer you as bad, not good. As something to be endured and borne, not enjoyed."

And so we have.

19

Sacrifice

I desire mercy, not sacrifice.

HOSEA 6:6; quoted by Jesus
in MATTHEW 9:13 and 12:7

WHENEVER I TALK ABOUT RETURNING TO FAITH after my years of atheism to the Christian college students I now teach, they always ask, Don't I miss it, the life I lived before I became a believer? Don't I miss my rowdy years abroad? They surmise, although I never tell the story this way, that those years must have amounted to pure joy and self-fulfillment—or, in any case, to a sexy, boozy freedom that they forego with reluctance. Raised in devout families and churches, they understand the life of faith looming before them largely as the pleasureless avoidance of behaviors in which others delight. Doing God's work, for them, means sacrifice.

Such thinking is not surprising. Although my students are familiar with the basic concept of grace—that salvation cannot be earned through human effort but is a free gift from God—they have also been exposed to the Bible from babyhood and know it for the rulebook it largely is.

That's, in any case, how the Bible seemed to me when I first read it. An instruction manual. And I was happy to find it so. Like the crowds that thronged around Jesus and the disciples, like the rich men and Pharisees who begged Jesus to tell them what they must do to enter God's kingdom, and like seemingly every church since those days, I wanted a clear set of dos and don'ts, a reliable recipe for God's approval and love.

Paradoxically, like my Christian students, I knew God's love did not depend on anything I did, good or bad. Neither my sacrifices nor my holy achievements. And I had learned the "filthy rags" philosophy underlying the teaching of the churches I attended: that humans are so incapable of avoiding sin that "all our righteous acts," as the prophet Isaiah puts it, "are like filthy rags" (64:6).

Scripture brims with the failings of devout believers. Abraham. David. Peter. Even Paul, his seeming self-righteousness notwithstanding, openly admits that he cannot do otherwise than sin. And again and again in my own daily life I discovered that these teachings were actually true. My attempts to do the right thing ended in failure. Or, occasionally, success contaminated by smug self-satisfaction. My attempts to resist doing evil were equally futile. My spiritual progress was hobbled by vile tendencies—arrogance, judgmentalism, self-centeredness, impatience, plain old meanness—and it frustrated and shamed me that I couldn't master these sins.

And, I was surprised and not a little disappointed to discover, the dos and don'ts didn't stop when one arrived at the New Testament. Read Jesus' famous Sermon on the Mount and you'll find listed, along with such obvious offenses as murder and adultery, every misbehavior you ever did or even thought about doing. Swearing, lusting, hating someone, calling someone a fool, you name it. And, in the midst of all the rule-slinging, Jesus warns, "Unless your righteousness surpasses that of the Pharisees and the teachers of the law, you will certainly not enter the kingdom of heaven" (Matthew 5:20).

The belief that earning God's approval means avoiding misconduct is ratified on every page of the Bible, Old Testament and New. It's no wonder that so many of us operate as though doing God's work is precisely the sacrificial life my students envision (and secretly dread): the staunch renouncement of forbidden pleasures on God's behalf and the pursuit of an alternative existence that's no fun.

Nestled among the rules and scary pronouncements, though, are the occasional suggestions that, paradoxically, such sacrifices *aren't* what God wants from us. When theological experts confront Jesus about what they see as his own inattentions to the letter of the Law, he advises them, on two separate occasions, to study God's own explanation of how to please him: "I desire mercy, not sacrifice" (Matthew 9:13; 12:7).

Mercy, not sacrifice, I thought when I first read those words. Here, finally, was a simple statement of what God wanted, and didn't want, from us.

As usual with Jesus' pronouncements, though, his meaning wasn't obvious. It seemed a strange dichotomy, first off: mercy and sacrifice hardly seemed like opposites. The notes in my study Bible said Jesus was quoting the prophet Hosea, so I went there first and found God speaking to the Israelites, complaining, "Your love is like the morning mist, like the early dew that disappears." Because of their fickleness, God tells them, "I cut you in pieces with my prophets" and "killed you with the words of my mouth. . . . For I desire mercy, not sacrifice, and acknowledgment of God rather than burnt offerings" (Hosea 6:4–6).

In context, Jesus' instruction was, if anything, less clear. What was expected of us, mercy toward others or love for God? The passage so bothered me that I looked it up in several translations and became even more confused. Hosea's word *love* that so easily evaporates was translated in other Bible versions as *goodness, loyalty*, and *kindness* and the *mercy* he desires as *faithfulness*, *duty*, and *loving-kindness*.

I eventually went out and bought an exhaustive concordance so as to look more closely at the Hebrew uses of the words in the passage and perhaps see a bit more clearly what Jesus meant. What I discovered astonished me. Although translated as two different words in most versions of Scripture—as *mercy* and *love* in the NIV—they were actually one and the same word in Hosea's Hebrew: the word חֶסֶד, *ḥesed*.

It was a common word in Scripture, I discovered upon further research, used in just about every book of the Old Testament and translated as everything from mercy and compassion to love, devotion, kindness, approval, and loyalty. With few exceptions— the passage from Hosea being one of them—the word was used to describe divine, not human, behavior. *Ḥesed* was, according to Hebrew rabbis who've debated the word's meaning for centuries, the epitome of loving-kindness, the kind of love God has toward us. What God wanted from us, according to Hosea, was to be loved the same way. To do the work of God, to live out one's faith, was not some ceremonial sacrifice or sacrificial avoidance of some forbidden pleasure but simply to love God back in the way God loved us.

The sacrificial (and unattainable) avoidance of sin my students aimed for, like the burnt sacrifices of the Old Testament, could not even approach the sort of love God has for us. Indeed, I don't think most of us would equate "sacrifice" with what we generally think of as "love." Love is a desirable emotion, something we *want* to do. Sacrifice, on the other hand, is by definition undesirable. To sacrifice is to forgo a desire for some higher purpose. Indeed, if we *want* to do something, we don't call it a sacrifice. We perform sacrifices out of duty, mostly, and with reluctance beforehand and regret afterward—the very reluctance and regret my students model when they envy my former freedom as a nonbeliever.

The Israelites probably experienced some of the same reluctance and regret in performing the sacrifices demanded by the Law. Having raised cattle—and knowing thus firsthand the hard work involved in ranching even today, with modern machinery, and the difficulty of making a living from it and how much hope one puts into one's best stock—I imagine it would have been difficult not to feel regret in passing the fattest, prettiest calves from one's herd on to some do-nothing priest to grill and consume on God's behalf. That's what some Israelites thought, I'm guessing. And imagine making grain and drink offerings, dumping your hard-earned produce out on a hot, greasy altar and watching it, literally, go up in steamy smoke. *What a waste!* I would have been thinking.

Which is probably something like what Cain thought, as he dutifully gathered up some of the harvest he had toiled so hard to produce. *I sweated and hacked at soil cursed with thistles and thorns, just as God said I would, and now God wants some of it back! It's not like God needs it or anything.*

And all the while God wanted something else entirely. Not our scowling obedience but *ḥesed*: to have his fondness for Cain returned the way babies unconsciously return their parents' affection. Wholly. Happily. Spontaneously.

Love—*ḥesed*, God's kind of love—is not driven by duty or rules, not by fairness or even logic. It is, in fact, not driven at all. Rather, it is shared and enjoyed.

20

The Work of the One God Sent

*I know that there is nothing better for people
than to be happy and to do good while they live. That
each of them may eat and drink, and find satisfaction
in all their toil—this is the gift of God.*

ECCLESIASTES 3:12–13

THE ONE GOD SENT WAS NOT DRIVEN. To be *driven* is to be forcibly compelled by some outside entity. Formed from the past participle of *drive*, the adjective *driven* is inherently passive in meaning. Ironically, though, those described as "driven" are by no means inactive. Synonyms for *driven* in contemporary usage include *obsessed, overburdened, compulsive, overworked*. To be driven is to exert oneself excessively and under duress, to labor so fanatically toward some end that one can't really enjoy oneself.

The One God Sent did work hard, it's true. In fact, during the three years of his work-life that comprise the Gospels, he did many jobs that others do for a living. He counseled, taught, adjudicated, fed, healed, and otherwise charitably assisted the crowds who surrounded him. Like Elijah before him (and doctors and EMT workers to this day), he revived several people from death. On one occasion, he vinted fine wine for a wedding party.

The One God Sent was also fueled by a force outside himself: "the power of the Spirit," as the Gospel writers frequently remind us. In public prayers, Jesus often pointed out that he was not acting on his own but in the name of his Father. Even his inherent goodness he ascribed not to himself or any action he performed but to God. Asked, "Good teacher . . . what must I do to inherit eternal life?" he responds, "Why do you call me good? . . . No one is good—except God alone" (Mark 10:17–18; also Luke 18:19).

And the One God Sent did have a very clear purpose that animated and inspired his work, which he formally announced early on in his ministry. Standing up in synagogue, he read it to his neighbors from "the scroll of the prophet Isaiah":

"The Spirit of the Lord is on me,
because he has anointed me
    to proclaim good news to the poor.
    He has sent me to proclaim freedom for the prisoners
    and recovery of sight for the blind,
    to set the oppressed free,
to proclaim the year of the Lord's favor." (Luke 4:18–19)

The prophet's words, he confirmed upon sitting back down, *were* his purpose: "Today this scripture is fulfilled in your hearing" (Luke 4:21), he concluded.

To deepen our understanding of the work of God, it's instructive, I think, to look closely at this earthly job description of the One God Sent. There is some recognizable work here—namely, proclaiming good news and freeing the oppressed—but none of Jesus' many other good works of those three busy years are specifically laid out in this mission statement. There's no plan to heal or counsel or feed, no promise to raise people from the dead, no proviso that he will undertake to relieve anyone's suffering except the cryptic announcement that he'll "set the oppressed free."

Jesus' statement of purpose is, in fact, much less inclusive than the scriptural passage he read from. In Isaiah's description of the year of the Lord's favor, the anointed one—that is, the Messiah—has lots more work before him: not merely proclaiming good news and freeing the oppressed but binding up the "brokenhearted," comforting "all who mourn," and providing for, releasing, and encouraging the wretched.

I once attended a church whose sole pastor frequently pointed out that he considered only teaching his job, not "pastoring"—by which he meant visiting the sick, counseling struggling couples, sending flowers to those in mourning, finding new members, organizing fellowship events, paying the bills, or doing the myriad other time- and spirit-consuming responsibilities that often overburden ministers. At the time, I attributed this pastor's abdication of his pastorly duties to laziness, and I was not alone in my thinking.

"All he has to do is prepare one sermon a week!" someone invariably murmured as we took on another chore or, more often, assigned yet more tasks to the already overburdened deacons and deacons' wives, who did most of the work that enabled the church to remain a church.

Jesus' work—though he did perform many duties that this pastor disdained—was fairly narrowly defined from the outset. God did not send him to feed *all* the poor in Palestine or even in his hometown or at his church or heal *all* the sick or release *every* prisoner or comfort *every* person mourning the death of a loved one. Rather, the work of the One God Sent was to proclaim good news—Freedom! Sight! God's favor!—and to free the oppressed, two tasks which I would argue are the same.

Consider the word *oppressed*. The Greek word for *oppressed* in Jesus' mission statement—θραύω, *thrauō*, the root of the English word *traumatize*—means *crushed, broken, torn*. In English, according to the *Merriam-Webster Dictionary*, *oppress* means "to crush or burden by abuse of power or authority" and "to burden spiritually or mentally: weigh heavily upon." Synonyms for *oppress* often evoke weight or burdens: *overload, encumber, saddle, weigh heavily upon*. Antonyms, strikingly, are not merely verbs about lessening or removing the burden—*aid, help, boost*—but verbs about being happy, like *hearten, gladden, delight*. The work of the One God Sent was to offer good news, especially the most delightful news of all: freedom from the heavy burden of trying to earn God's favor.

Jesus came not to further burden us but to unload the heavy burden we misunderstand to be God's work. He makes this clear in condemning "experts in the law," saying, "Woe to you, because you load people down with burdens they can hardly carry, and you yourselves will not lift one finger to help them" (Luke 11:46). Jesus' good news, the best news there could be, is that God's work isn't a burden at all. It is, rather, the ultimate *freedom* from burdens: God's age-old promise of rest!

As the human embodiment of God's Word, the One God Sent naturally proclaimed God's good news in the most effective way a message can be communicated: by modeling. In the Gospels, we see Jesus hemmed in by crowds of needy followers, healing one after the next, but we as often see him attending dinner parties, barbecuing fish on the beach, taking walks with his buddies, and escaping "to a solitary place" for alone-time and prayer.

Jesus didn't set out to heal or help every needy person he encountered or even every person who asked for help. He also voiced some rather shocking constraints on what he was willing to do. When a Canaanite woman asked him to heal her demon-possessed daughter, he told her, "I was sent only to the lost sheep of Israel"

(Matthew 15:24). Even after she knelt before him and wailed, "Lord, help me!" he still balked, saying, "It is not right to take the children's bread and toss it to the dogs" (Matthew 15:25–26). Although he did eventually give in and help the woman, the limitations he set for himself are evident.

The One God Sent healed and helped on his own terms, not anyone else's. He healed a deaf and mute man some people brought him—but only after he "took him aside, away from the crowd" (Mark 7:33), thus thwarting the people's evident plan to make the miracle a public event. In response to demands for a miraculous healing in story after story, he offered instead forgiveness from sins. In other stories, he healed people or released them from demons without even being asked. In one instance, he encountered a widow whose only son had died, and "his heart went out to her" (Luke 7:13). Unbidden, he comforted her, touched the coffin, and spoke the boy back to life. God's work—if Jesus' many miracles were representative of it, as I believe they were—should be something we *want* to do, he repeatedly demonstrated, not something we feel pressured or driven to do.

In other words, God's work should please the worker, not just the needy ones who stand to benefit from the work. Or, to revisit how Paul puts it, "Each of you should give what you have decided in your heart to give, not reluctantly or under compulsion, for God loves a cheerful giver" (2 Corinthians 9:7).

This is surely gladdening news. What we do is up to us! We should not feel under any compulsion—not driven!—to do some overwhelming amount of work on God's behalf but only what makes us happy!

Sadly, though, instead of being gladdened by Paul's words, I find myself unconsciously adding cheerfulness to my imagined spiritual load. *I am not cheerful enough when I spend time with Mamaw*, I chide myself. *I need to somehow make myself enjoy this work.* Carrying on a daily conversation with someone who is

sinking fast into dementia and won't wear hearing aids and repeats her own vague stories and questions incessantly and whose
conversational world has shrunk to the size of a three-year-old's is
hard enough, I protest inwardly. Feeling cheerful about it is more
than I can bear. Thus I turn the good news that God wants me to
enjoy myself into yet another load heaped upon the burden of
God's work, and my inevitable failure to be cheerful taints my
charitable work with bitterness.

Successful completion of a task undertaken in God's name results in joy, not bitterness. Nowhere is this principle as plain to me
as in Jesus' story of the lost sheep. The shepherd is so upset at his
loss that he abandons his main flock "in the open country" to go in
search of the one.

If you have never been involved in animal husbandry, you can't
know what a big job going after that one sheep probably was for
that shepherd—involving not only risk to the rest of the flock but
an unwelcome interruption of other necessary duties to lurch
from field to field looking for one seemingly invisible animal.

And then to catch it! My husband and I have chased more than
one single calf for days before finally managing to corner it and
drive it back to the paddock where it belonged. But the shepherd
in Jesus' story is so intent on the sheep's safety that he seems unaware of his effort. He feels no compulsion. He just does it.

"And when he finds it," we're told, "he joyfully puts it on his
shoulders and goes home. Then he calls his friends and neighbors
together and says, 'Rejoice with me; I have found my lost sheep'"
(Luke 15:5-6). Joyfully. Rejoice. Doing God's work should result
in sheer joy.

Thus, when Jesus sent out seventy-two disciples as "workers
into his harvest field," they "returned with joy and said, 'Lord,
even the demons submit to us in your name'" (Luke 10:2, 17).
Jesus was also "full of joy" and praised his Father that, in his
words, "this is what you were pleased to do" (Luke 10:21).

Jesus' mission is not to oppress believers but to transform them into jubilant workers for God, and the work they do is all about joy. As Jesus tells his disciples, following his primary command to "Love each other" as he loves them will have the result that his joy may be in them and their "joy may be complete" (John 15:11–12).

Though obedient to his Father, Jesus never worked under compulsion. His three years of modeling what God's work could look like for us reveal healthy limitations on what he undertook to accomplish. And the result was never bitterness or stress but unqualified joy.

21

Woe to Us

*Jesus replied, "And you experts in the law,
woe to you, because you load people down with
burdens they can hardly carry, and you yourselves
will not lift one finger to help them."*

LUKE 11:46

UNDERSTANDING GOD'S WORK AS LESS BURDENSOME than
people usually imagine it—as, indeed, something one should enjoy
and that, even then, should be limited to keep it from becoming
burdensome—is hardly a popular sermon topic. It's more rhetorically satisfying, for one thing, to promote grand acts of holiness or
sacrifice than to examine the small print of the biblical laws and
counsel moderation in our spiritual work-lives. When the parents
of a murdered child forgive the unrepentant murderer, for example, it's all over the news. We find such large pieties more impressive than more reasonable acts of mercy—the kind God
himself models—in which forgiveness is predicated on the wrongdoer's recognition of the crime and heartfelt repentance.

Also, churches need their congregants' holy efforts and sacrificial offerings in order to survive. Promoting limits on congregants' contributions rather than spurring them on to do and give more would be organizationally risky.

So, a sermon on tithing, for example, is likelier to differentiate a tithe from spontaneous charitable donations and stipulate that the tithe *must* go to one's church and *must* be a regular and routine contribution—and thus dependable income, from the church's perspective—than to focus on that 10 percent cap mentioned in the commandments about tithing. If the 10 percent limit is mentioned at all, it will probably be in the context of a remark that the tithe should be *at least* 10 percent of one's *gross*, not net, income or that, as I have heard preached more than once, the 10 percent should be regarded as the "bare minimum" one should give. Given that preachers derive their salaries from tithes, it is unlikely that they will expound on the merits of that 10 percent cap—how it can free the giver from the tension that money considerations often cause and make giving away one's money an enjoyable experience—much less that they will actively discourage congregants from exceeding 10 percent.

Similarly, a sermon on the commandment that we "Remember the Sabbath day" is likelier to generalize the "keeping it holy" (Exodus 20:8) part to mean undertake holy projects than to dawdle in the lengthy explanation that follows the Sabbath mandate detailing what form this holiness is actually supposed to take: namely, that "you shall not do any work, neither you, nor your son or daughter, nor your male or female servant, nor your animals, nor any foreigner residing in your towns. For in six days the LORD made the heavens and the earth, the sea, and all that is in them, but he rested on the seventh day" (Exodus 20:10–11).

Many of the typical believer's Sunday behaviors might be regarded as holy, but such activities often constitute anything but rest. Anything but, in fact, a *Sabbath* in the word's original sense.

Instead of resting or ceasing, we spend our Sabbaths in ceaseless activity: not only church attendance but the countless worthy activities that go on before and during and between and after the services: driving buses to pick up the elderly, buying doughnuts, setting up for the fellowship hour, teaching Sunday school classes, running children's church, ushering, organizing building campaign events, counting money and working on the church budget, participating in evangelism projects and weekly food giveaways, preparing dishes for and setting up and cleaning up after the potluck, overseeing myriad children's activities, contributing to and running the church rummage sale.

"You should lead the adult class," a former student sitting next to me at church recently whispered. "You're such a good teacher!" *But I need a day of resting! Not teaching. Not working. Not doing anything!* I thought emphatically, desperately. I didn't want to make her feel bad, though, and the music was starting anyway, so I said nothing. All Sunday long and late into that night, I fantasized about actually getting to enjoy God's weekly gift to us: a mandated rest.

That's how God phrases the command to rest on the Sabbath, as a *gift*: "How long will you refuse to keep my commands and my instructions?" God asks the Israelites in the desert. "Bear in mind that the LORD has *given* you the Sabbath" (Exodus 16:28–29, my emphasis). God's original work assignment that humans till the soil of Eden—a task much more arduous after our expulsion from that lush, weedless garden—was accompanied by a sweet benefits package: a weekly vacation from our labors.

This day of not working *is* sometimes honored. I know elderly people who don't use household appliances on Sunday. And, in some Judeo-Christian communities, stores and other businesses—especially unholy ones like liquor stores—close on the Sabbath. And once, when I lived in New Orleans, I took a bicycle trip on a Sunday and had a flat. None of the stores that were open that day would sell me the wrench I needed to fix my bike and continue my trip, because local blue laws forbade the selling of tools on the Sabbath.

My husband tells of how, growing up, he was forbidden (or forbade himself, as he sometimes tells it, reluctant to blame his parents for such an absurdity) to do anything even remotely worklike on Sunday. He couldn't build Lincoln Log houses or paint the model Messerschmitt he had finished gluing together the week before. Building and painting were work, even in play.

Similarly, in a chapter entitled "Sundays" in Laura Ingalls Wilder's autobiographical *Little House in the Big Woods*, the Ingalls girls' Sabbaths were rigorously regulated. They weren't allowed to run or make noise or even sew or knit doll clothes. Instead they had to "sit quietly" while their mother read to them. Sundays passed so slowly and so pleasurelessly that they could hardly bear them. As a result, for Laura and her sister Mary, the Day of Rest was not a gift at all. After getting in trouble for playing with their dog, Jack, Laura snaps at her father that she hates Sundays. The Ingalls household keeps the Sabbath holy not merely by not working or by resting but by not playing, not making noise, not enjoying themselves.

God's work—and most especially the assignment to rest from work—is designed to be easy. Pleasurable even. But for some reason we refuse to have it so. Indeed, many of us worry that "getting anything out of" any godly undertaking—weight loss from fasting, thanks or recognition for a kindness, enjoyment from exercising one's skills—somehow cancels out the work's spiritual value.

A colleague of mine was once outraged that fellow faculty he'd asked to teach special workshops in addition to their regular full-time jobs balked at doing so without being paid.

"But it's our mission to serve students!" he railed. "You're not supposed to make money from mission work!"

I've even heard preachers discourage congregants from regarding their natural talents—skills they are good at and enjoy exercising—as their spiritual gifts. The spiritual gifts are not for our benefit—not opportunities to enjoy using our God-given talents—they argue, but sacrificial duties to others, made the more onerous by the widely preached counsel that we should work especially hard on developing the spiritual gifts that we *aren't* already good at and *don't* enjoy.

How did it come to be that believers turn some of God's best gifts to us—not just our talents and interests and that lovely day of rest once a week but the lenience and clemency built into virtually every godly work assignment—into another joyless task to be accomplished, another heavy stone upon our backs? How did we come to expect and even demand that the easy work of God be sacrificial and unenjoyable?

The Bible offers many examples of those so obsessed with the Law that they turn it into a punishment, notably the Pharisees and legal experts, groups so commonly spoken of together in the Gospels that they seem synonymous. The word *pharisaical* has come to mean legalist to a fault. Though the most scripturally literate of their time, legal experts of the New Testament consistently misread God's expectations as a set of petty rules apparently designed to plague people into holiness. Jesus didn't wash his hands before eating, they pointed out, and they faulted him for tending to the sick on the Day of Rest and strolling with his friends through grain fields, collecting handfuls of kernels from the standing grain to chomp on as they went.

We often interpret the Pharisees' habit of turning the Bible's commands into a nitpicky obstacle course as a ruse to entrap Jesus, but the Pharisees made the same demands of everyone around them, as Jesus points out in a sermon condemning their hypocrisy, their pretentiousness, their sloth, and, most especially, their habit of weighing others down with rules.

But Jesus' sermon addresses not the Pharisees and teachers of the law but those whom they oppressed: the crowds who followed him. And, before criticizing the spiritual experts' behavior of burdening others with rules, Jesus first goes out of his way to legitimize these experts' status as God's representatives: "The teachers of the law and the Pharisees sit in Moses' seat," Jesus tells the crowds. "So you must be careful to do everything they tell you. But do not do what they do, for they do not practice what they preach" (Matthew 23:2–3).

Elsewhere in the Gospels, Jesus mocks the Pharisees' legal obsessiveness—that, for example, they tithe 10 percent of the herbs on their windowsills while ignoring "justice and the love of God"—and he comments that they "should have practiced the latter without leaving the former undone" (Luke 11:42). Their preoccupation with every jot and tittle of the Law is not technically wrong, Jesus seems to be saying, just wrongheaded. There seems, in other words, to be a rightness to these teachers' holy impulses, even the impulse to pay attention to such scriptural minutia as the tithing of mint and basil. But somehow, in carrying out these impulses, they circumvent the spirit of the Law: the love and justice God breathed into it.

In what is surely the worst accusation in this sermon, Jesus backhandedly commends Israel's teachers for traveling "over land and sea to win a single convert" while in the same breath lamenting, "when you have succeeded, you make them twice as much a child of hell as you are" (Matthew 23:15).

Children of hell. I think many of us believers and our own converts might be so identified, caught up, as we so often are, in the dreadful burden of trying to do and make others do what we have decided is the right thing. Like the Pharisees and teachers of the law, we cling to the stress and guilt from which we were freed by ratcheting up the easy burden of loving God and others into impossibly stressful and guilt-inspired über-rules for moral living.

The 10 percent tithe becomes the bare minimum. The obligation to forgive whenever a brother or sister comes and asks for forgiveness becomes forgive every wrong always, immediately, and whether or not the wrongdoer repents. Love your neighbor as yourself becomes love *everyone* and love them *better than* yourself—or, as a colleague of mine preaches it, "Like everybody."

There is, as Jesus says of the Pharisees' holy practices, nothing inherently wrong with any of these impulses. Most are supported by Scripture. And liking everyone and giving everything you have to the poor and forgiving all wrongs are certainly great and holy goals.

They're just not realistic or achievable goals. And as such, they result not in contentment but in heavy, cumbersome loads of guilt and stress and long histories of failure that we tie on to our own and others' shoulders. We feel them there, weighing us down, hampering our progress. But, since we cannot see them, we never think to take Jesus at his word and let him help us lighten our load.

Sometimes I wonder if we're not in fact trying to *outdo* God with our holy efforts. God goes on holiday after six days of hard work, honoring both the work and its cessation; we turn that holiday into a holy workday governed by spirit-stifling behavioral rules. God forgives those who are sorry for their sins, but we aspire to forgive *everyone*, no matter what.

In any case, by complicating God's simple recipe for contentment into ever more stringent rules for holiness involving heavy duties and joyless sacrifice, we attempt to achieve God's love through arduous effort instead of taking up the nearly effortless godly work that is our assignment: simply believing ever more deeply in the One God Sent.

"Woe to you!" Jesus might say to many of us today, just as he did to the Pharisees and teachers of the law. And he would be right. The burdens we heap upon ourselves and others are likely to achieve little and burn us out, bringing us nothing but woe.

22

Knock Yourself Out!

Jesus answered, "If you want to be perfect, go, sell your possessions and give to the poor, and you will have treasure in heaven. Then come, follow me."

MATTHEW 19:21

ONCE A STUDENT WITH LIMITED ENGLISH complained to me that his American roommate got irritated whenever he came back to their room and found my student studying. My student made a gesture of piqued surprise to show me how his roommate acted and said, mimicking the guy's voice, "Wow, you're really knocking yourself out!"

"What he mean by that?" my student asked me.

He guessed the guy was threatening to hurt him or telling him to do damage to himself, and I took pains to explain that no, there was probably no threat involved—unless my student was picking up on nonverbal cues that he hadn't demonstrated to me.

"Knocking yourself out," I explained, was simply an idiomatic expression referring to unnecessary or over-the-top exertions. "He thought you were trying to be perfect," I said.

If I were to write one of those Bible translations that come out every so often in which everything is rendered in contemporary English, that's what I'd have Jesus say to that rich young man who wants to know "what good thing" he needs to accomplish in order to "get eternal life" (Matthew 19:16). The guy's been following the commandments his whole life, he assures Jesus, but somehow he thinks that's not enough.

"Whoa! Knock yourself out, why don't you!" Jesus would exclaim in my version of the Bible in lieu of the milder "If you want to be perfect . . ." (Matthew 19:21). And the guy would go away sad—not merely because, as the text explains, "he had great wealth" (Matthew 19:22) and didn't want to part with it, although that was certainly part of his problem, but because he sensed himself under attack from the very person who he thought had all the answers.

And in truth, the young man *did* want to be perfect. But what was wrong with that? Scripture, as he understood it—indeed, as many understand it to this day—was one big demand for perfection. Surely perfection was what God *wanted* of us. Why was Jesus making fun of someone who was just trying to do what God wanted?

Indeed, perhaps the man had been present at the Sermon on the Mount, where Jesus himself demanded such morally impeccable behavior as turning the other cheek when attacked or gouging out one's eyes if attracted to someone besides one's spouse or, if tempted to steal, chopping off one's own hand.

"Be perfect, therefore, as your heavenly Father is perfect" (Matthew 5:48), Jesus concluded his litany of hyperboles.

I envision the poor guy as he walked away. Soon his sadness was replaced by ire, I'm guessing. Before he had taken twenty steps, I'll bet he was already totting up all the rumors he'd heard of this Jesus dining with rich people and tax collectors, clearly leading the good life. *Hypocrite*, I could hear the guy deciding, or trying to decide, about this guru of the Jews.

So, the young man would sadly (and probably a little angrily) return home and resume the strangely unsatisfying life of holy striving he'd been leading before his conversation with Jesus.

God is certainly perfect, I could imagine him reasoning as he went about his holy life, and humans were made in God's image. Clearly perfectionism should be our goal in seeking to please God.

But nothing could be less true.

Here's the trouble with the pursuit of perfection: It impedes one's progress and undermines any work one can hope to achieve. Even the holy work we do to please God.

According to cognitive psychologists, perfectionism underlies a host of mental illnesses, everything from depression and anxiety to obsessive-compulsiveness, addictions, and eating disorders. One might expect perfectionism would at least cause a person to be more industrious and productive, but this isn't so. In the workplace, perfectionism reduces productivity, elevates stress, and causes relational problems between coworkers.

A key factor in perfectionists' failure as workers is that they set goals for themselves that they can't possibly achieve—that no one can achieve—and thus set themselves up to fail. Secretly, perfectionists know they can't achieve their impossible goals, so many develop a debilitating habit of procrastination. In my courses, I often have smart and capable students who never turn anything in on time—and sometimes don't turn in anything at all—because nothing they do is as perfect as they want it to be.

Alternatively, some perfectionists pursue their unachievable goals so obsessively that they become workaholics, crippled by stress and pernicious self-doubt. They work so much and so hard that they damage everything important to them—family, friendship, recreation—and eventually burn out even on the work they care so much about. As a result, they are chronically dissatisfied.

The pursuit of perfection is, in short, not conducive to healthy and productive work. Perfectionism undoes what little it achieves.

Some scholars make a distinction between "good perfectionism"—the pursuit of excellence—and "bad perfectionism," the destructive kind I've been describing. But the pursuit of excellence and the pursuit of perfection differ in a definitive way: Excellence is achievable, at least on a small scale; perfection is not. To pursue perfection is to fail—unless you are God. But we are not God.

I think that's what Jesus was getting at in his weird initial response to the rich guy's question about "what good thing" he must do to "get eternal life": "Why do you ask me about what is good?" Jesus replied. "There is only One who is good. If you want to enter life, keep the commandments" (Matthew 19:16–17). In other words, we may be made in God's image, but we are not God. Only God is perfect. We are not expected to do more or harder work than God has assigned. In trying to be "good," as the young man understands it—that is, perfect—we are trying to *be* God.

This was not an easy idea to understand, even for Jesus' disciples. After the young man sadly leaves, the disciples seem as aghast as the young man himself, even more so when Jesus remarks, "Children, how hard it is to enter the kingdom of God!" (Mark 10:24).

"Who then can be saved?" they murmur to one another (Mark 10:26), and Jesus has to explain: "With man this is impossible, but not with God; all things are possible with God" (Mark 10:27).

Perfectionists have a hard time doing God's work—that is, simply believing in the One God Sent—because they are bent on doing more. Only perfection is enough, but they are incapable of perfection, and knowing they can't be perfect weighs them down and hinders their progress. For them, the burden of God's work is particularly heavy.

The young man's wealth—and Jesus' own assessment of wealth as an impediment to spiritual progress—slants most interpretations of this story. But, consider. As believers in the One God Sent, we are all rich. Not monetarily, maybe—although many of us who would not call ourselves rich are amazingly wealthy in the global context—but certainly in terms of the good things available to us: God's love despite our imperfections and forgiveness when we fail; our life on this earth, which even believers are reluctant to relinquish; and potentially, as Jesus says in the lavish language of the King James Version, the "many mansions" of heaven, where Jesus is preparing a place for us (John 14:2).

Not to mention the gift of Scripture itself: a no-fail plan for how to get there. God gave us commandments that make it easy for us to succeed. And in story after story, from patriarchs and prophets to Peter and Paul, we find obvious human failures—adulterers, murderers, doubters, narcissists, raging dogmatists—who, in the words of the writer of Hebrews, "were all commended for their faith" and even "pleased God" (Hebrews 11:39 and 11:5).

By twisting the work of God into something more than it needs to be—something *more* than mere faith, with more exacting rules—perfectionists spit in the face of such commendations and reject God's unearned, unearnable pleasure, although they want both desperately. Worse—if anything can be worse than failing to please God—perfectionists believe they are doing just the opposite. They think the loads they suffer under are winning God's approval and getting them to heaven. In reality, their loads are so ponderous and cumbersome that they struggle to take even the smallest step forward. In knocking themselves out, they risk knocking themselves out of the running entirely.

Doing God's work the way Jesus recommends—that is, merely believing in the One God Sent—should be easy, not hard. If it's not easy, something's wrong.

This is not to say that some believers will not suffer dreadfully in living out their faith. Some will. But even in such cases, Jesus promises that the work of believing in the One God Sent will be, on some level, effortless and that we can get the job done, to our and God's satisfaction.

In all three versions of the story of the rich young man offered in the Gospels, the writers go out of their way to say that Jesus "looked at" the young man and later "looked at" his disciples before answering their question, "Who then can be saved?"

Elsewhere in the Gospels when we're expressly told that Jesus "looked at" someone, he seems to be experiencing intense emotion. When Peter denies him the third time, for example, "The Lord turned and looked straight at Peter" (Luke 22:61). And when Jesus meets a man with a shriveled hand in the synagogue with the Pharisees watching, eager to accuse him, "He looked around at them in anger and, deeply distressed at their stubborn hearts, said to the man, 'Stretch out your hand'" (Mark 3:5). Jesus' distress—that is, his hope for Peter, for the Pharisees, for every last one of us—must have been conveyed in his probing looks.

In Mark's account of the rich man, in any case, after the young man reports that he has kept the commandments since he was a boy, we're told that "Jesus looked at him and loved him" (Mark 10:21). Seconds later, the man will fail Jesus, just as the Pharisees and even Peter failed Jesus at crucial moments and as we all do much of the time. The love Jesus had for that man predated his failure, though. It also survived it. Jesus *still* loves that man. His love, in other words, is not dependent on our perfection or even on our attempts at perfection. It's dependent entirely on our willingness to let Jesus perfect us.

The adjective *perfect* in Jesus' response to the young man—and in his demand that we "Be perfect" as our "heavenly Father is perfect" (Matthew 5:48)—may also be translated as mature or finished. It is derived the Greek noun τέλος (*telos*), which means completion, accomplishment, consummation, and fulfillment—literally, a goal that has been achieved. Some versions of Scripture translate Jesus' words in Matthew's version of the story not as "If you want to be perfect" but rather as something like "If you wish to be complete" (Matthew 19:21 NASB), making Jesus' response more or less synonymous with what Mark remembered Jesus saying to the young man: "One thing you lack" (Mark 10:21). That "one thing" was the last part of Jesus' recommendation to the young man: following him.

Perfection isn't God's goal in giving us rules to follow. As the writer of Hebrews asserts, "the law made nothing perfect" (Hebrews 7:19). Not even the Levitical priests, who knew the law better than anyone else and devoted their lives to carrying it out, could achieve perfection. For, "If perfection could have been attained," then "why was there still need for another priest to come"—namely, Jesus? (Hebrews 7:11).

To be perfect, to be complete, all we lack is the One God Sent in the yoke beside us. And he is already there, already pulling for us. Already, since the beginning of time, gazing over at us in love.

23

The Bible Says

*All Scripture is God-breathed and is useful
for teaching, rebuking, correcting and training in
righteousness, so that the servant of God may be
thoroughly equipped for every good work.*

2 TIMOTHY 3:16–17

FOR MANY CHRISTIANS, THE SIMPLE TASK of believing in the
One God Sent and responding freely to that belief is complicated
by, well, the Bible itself. After all, the Bible—both New Testament
and Old—is packed with meticulous commands to do this and not
do that and compelling accounts of the consequences of disobedience. As such, many believers exert themselves to believe, not in
the One God Sent, but in the Bible itself.

Consider. Despite my husband's avowal, while I was yet an
atheist, that the only commandments he really tried to follow were
to love God and love his neighbor as himself, my initial scrutiny of
his peculiar faith, as I saw it, revealed a man rigidly observant of
what seemed to me the most trifling scriptural rules. Kris prayed,

on his knees, in our walk-in closet—having imbibed from the King James Version of the Bible read to him in early childhood the injunction, "When thou prayest, enter into thy closet, and when thou hast shut thy door, pray to thy Father which is in secret" (Matthew 6:6 KJV).

To Kris's child mind, a closet was a closet. Even though he later came to understand the difference between King James' Renaissance English and modern usage and by then routinely read a version of Scripture that translated "thy closet" as "your room"— and even though he was able to articulate these distinctions to someone as unfamiliar with the Bible as I was in those days—nevertheless he continued to follow the scriptural command as he had understood it in childhood regarding the appropriate locus of his conversations with God. I learned to avoid the closet when I thought the Spirit might be upon him.

Kris also took to heart Scripture's various vague injunctions against foul language. In the graduate creative writing program where we met, Kris was the only avowed Christian. Though admired among our non-Christian—mostly *anti*-Christian—peers for his dark and sometimes crude short stories, he never used or even implied foul language in his writing, much less in real life. To this day, when he recounts some bawdy tale told by one of his clients, he whispers single-letter substitutions for any objectionable words or else omits them entirely.

Our occupation in those days was farming—liquid work, I quickly learned, that filled the container of each day and not infrequently spilled over into the next day and the next. Our work had no beginning, middle, or end. No matter how hard we toiled or how much we got done in the course of a day, there were always heifers to check on or fences to build or fix or paint or pond ice to break and no end to weeds to be brushhogged or poisoned or equipment to be maintained or repaired or bought new. For farmers, as far as I could tell, there was no such thing as a day off.

With one exception: Unless we had some absolutely un-put-off-able emergency—hay down and dry and ready to bale and rain on the horizon or else a literal ox in the ditch (or, more likely, a hysterical heifer trotting the pasture margins with a big-boned calf dangling from her hind end)—we *never* worked on Sunday. Not, mind you, because we went to church in those days. No, we couldn't work on Sunday, Kris told me, because, according to the Bible, it was the Day of Rest. I didn't argue. God knows we needed the rest.

To the faith-outsider I was then, Kris's faith amounted to obedience to a set of often crazy-seeming rules learned in childhood— like the rules my daughters would later learn at the churches we attended. Every Sunday school discussion they reported to me was about behavioral matters. On one classroom wall was a Ten Commandment-style list of things forbidden for Christian teens: alcohol, sex, disrespecting one's elders, immodest dress, etc. The churches we attended were all founded on the good news that Jesus had died for our sins, but the focus of their teaching, both in these classes and from the pulpit, was mostly on the bad news that we should just be good and not need Jesus' sacrifice in the first place.

Don't misunderstand me. I am not saying that living the Christian life doesn't involve following behavioral rules. It does— even for a gung-ho *sola scriptura* believer like me. I rely on the Bible to help me live my life, and the Bible is full of rules. Doing my best to follow them is certainly beneficial—both to me and to others. But obedience to these rules is not synonymous with doing the work of believing in the One God Sent.

The biblical writers, in what little they have to say about Scripture's role in the life of the believer, are unambiguous on this point. Certainly Israel's teachers promote obedience to God's "commands, decrees and laws"—a common string of synonyms throughout the Old Testament, redundant presumably for emphasis—as a means of ensuring longevity and prosperity in this life. These commandments, Moses explains upon disseminating them in the first place, enable those who obey them to "enjoy long life" and also ensure that "it may go well with" them and that they "may increase greatly in a land flowing with milk and honey" (Deuteronomy 6:2–3). New Testament writers—writing well before their own writings were added to what was then thought of as "Scripture"—recommend Scripture as a tool for doing God's work, not as the work itself. Scripture equips "the servant of God," as Paul writes, "for every good work" (2 Timothy 3:16–17)—especially the best work of all: to believe in the One God Sent.

However, the apostle Peter assures us that God "has given us everything we need for a godly life through our knowledge of him who called us by his own glory and goodness" (2 Peter 1:3). Scripture, he concedes a few lines later, is "completely reliable" and worthy of our attention, but it is at best "a light shining in a dark place" compared to the dawning of day that is Jesus (2 Peter 1:19). To paraphrase Peter here, to do God's work, all we need is knowledge of the One God Sent. Certainly the Bible informs this knowledge and equips us for holy living, but to equate God's work with mere obedience to biblical commands is like equating a house with the hammers and saws used to build it.

Jesus routinely referred to Scripture as the account of himself. In his very first sermon, he read from the prophet Isaiah and then said of what he had read, "Today this scripture is fulfilled in your hearing" (Luke 4:21). Later he cautioned, "You study the Scriptures diligently because you think that in them you have eternal life. These are the very Scriptures that testify about me, yet you refuse to come to me to have life" (John 5:39–40).

Coming to Jesus. No greater work is required of us.

PART 4

Getting to Ease

24

Entering God's Rest

So then, a sabbath rest still remains for the people
of God; for those who enter God's rest also cease
from their labors as God did from his.
Let us therefore make every
effort to enter that rest.

Hebrews 4:9–11 NRSV

ONCE I HAPPENED UPON A LIST OF ALL the kinds of "work" traditionally forbidden among Jews on the Sabbath. Referred to as the "39 *Melachot*"—the "39 Labors"—it covers every imaginable work of biblical days. Predictable inclusions are the farmer's tasks—sowing, plowing, reaping—and such household chores as spinning and cooking. Professional occupations of the time—like writing, building and weaving—and even the undoing of such activities (erasing, demolishing, unraveling) also make the list.

Some items on the list describe more general exertions—such as planning, deciding, and finishing—that differentiate work from the rest one should enjoy on the Sabbath. Think about the mindset you are in when you think, *If only I could figure out what to do next* or *I sure wish someone else would make up my mind for me* or *I just want to get this done,* and you will understand what the "39 Labors" are all about: a weekly, twenty-four-hour respite, not merely from the chores of daily living but from stress in general. A rest, not just from laboring but from *thinking* about laboring. And from the ever-tempting pull toward accomplishment.

The Gospels reference these "39 Labors" whenever Jesus is taken to task for picking grain or healing people on the Sabbath. Indeed, Jesus' telling the sick man at the pool of Bethesda to pick up his mat and walk amounted, in essence, to his telling the man to violate what rabbinical experts of his day and ever since saw as the central task of the "39 Labors": carrying any burden at all on the Sabbath. This quintessential forbidden work—taking a burden upon oneself in any way—represents for rabbinical scholars humankind's overweening urge to master the created world and thus outdo God.

As I read about this notion of carrying as an exertion one might need a rest from now and then, the image that immediately came to my mind was of carrying a child. On the one hand, it could be a delightful task: carrying a mewing newborn proudly into the admiring presence of one's acquaintance. When new moms show up, babe in arms, at my university, we all lean in and coo in pleasure and longing. Passing students beg to hold the baby. *Oh, if only one could return to that moment!* those of us with grown children think. The funny little purplish face staring up at me. The smell of baby. Her sweet, warm, weightless presence—finally arrived after the nine long months of anticipation!—against my shoulder.

On the other hand, even that glad task of carrying could become burdensome. Ever since my daughters were born, I have found carrying them—first literally, then figuratively—to be my primary work. I managed to delay both girls' sitting and walking times by lugging them around on my hip well into their toddling years.

Later, their worlds of diapers and books and toys and leaky sippy cups dangling heavily from my shoulder, I would drag them wailing from swimming pools and parks and libraries where we had already overstayed our planned enjoyment. Even now, with both Charlotte and Lulu in college and largely independent, I find myself carrying them continuously—their troubles, their misdeeds, their plans. I stress about them in the night, when I should be sleeping. And I don't expect to be done with this burden of carrying them anytime soon. *Woman over nature,* I reflected as I read the ancient rabbis' teaching. *I'm trying to be God.*

Interestingly, though, I learned as I read on, carrying one's child is implicitly excluded from the *39 Melachot* by the stipulation that only public, not private, carrying is forbidden. *Since babies would have been attended to primarily in the home in biblical days,* I thought heavily, hauling them from room to room—from lap-time to play-time to time-out to nap-time to bed—would thus have been an exception to the Sabbath rest. *Those poor Israelite moms,* I thought. *Every possible exertion prohibited except theirs.*

Before the word *sexist* managed to extricate itself from my musings, though, I was remembering every Bible story I had ever read that mentioned Israelite women's attitudes toward their babies. How they longed to have them! How proud they were when they did have them! How blessed they considered themselves to be as mothers!

I saw in my mind, again, Charlotte's newborn arms and later Lulu's, raised to my face, beckoning to me from my very first moments in their company. Soon after, I remembered, the baby would be clutching me, thus performing that mysterious defiance of gravity that happens when one carries a live and conscious being as opposed to a dead or inanimate burden. By sharing with me the burden of their weight, my babies became, in a sense, weightless. The rabbis of old, I decided, were onto something. Although carrying one's child could be onerous at times, it was not really work but, rather, sheer pleasure. To hold and be held. To desire. To be desired. The essential physical manifestations of our most longed-for condition: love.

It fascinates me how readily I allow my greatest joys in life, the two daughters God gave into my care, to become, in a selfish instant of self-pity, perceived burdens. How suddenly that odd little list of laws defining the world as I would have it—Thou shalt play happily and let me read my book; Thou shalt not want to stay at the park any longer than I do; Thou shalt not do any of the bad things I did when I was your age—temporarily supplants in my estimation all memory of the pleasure promised and received through my daughters' existence. What is this tendency to clutch at my rule—*This* is what a person should do. *This* is how to be happy!—over the child?

What is it about rules? Every church I have ever attended—even the ones who regard legalists as the worst sinners—seems to obsess about rules. Every sermon, wherever I go, offers some new strategy for living a godly life. Do this. Don't do that. And the bulletins handed out at the beginning of the services list countless opportunities to take up the burden of God's work. We should pray for this one, donate money to that one, help with Vacation Bible School, serve. We are surrounded by needy others. The farther in the distance we look, the more calls on our Christian duty there are out there, mission prospects layered as thickly as the stars on a clear night. We should give of ourselves, our money, our time. And those who don't do whatever it is—as I once heard preached of failing to attend church whenever the church doors were open—are in danger of losing their salvation.

Even God's explicit commandment *not* to work—that is, to rest: the fourth of the Ten Commandments, violation of which was punishable by death in Old Testament days (Exodus 35:2; Numbers 15:32–36)—we wring into yet more work, yet more rules to follow and things to do, our own countless *Melachots*. Consider this answer, in the Heidelberg Catechism used in my current church, to Question 103, "What does God require in the fourth commandment?":

> First, that the ministry of the gospel and the schools be maintained; (a) and that I, especially on the sabbath, that is, on the day of rest, diligently frequent the church of God, (b) to hear his word, (c) to use the sacraments, (d) publicly to call upon the Lord, (e) and contribute to the relief of the poor. (f) Secondly, that all the days of my life I cease from my evil works, and yield myself to the Lord, to work by his Holy Spirit in me: and thus begin in this life the eternal sabbath. (g)*

Ministry. Schools. Diligently. We're to go to church and contribute to the relief of the poor on Sunday and work by his Holy Spirit in us—whatever that might mean—all the days of our lives. Work, work, and more work. Resting once a week, in the Heidelberg Catechism, amounts to a lifetime of diligent exertions and avoidances. A lifetime of stress.

The work of God amounts to, if I let it, just such tasks and calls to righteousness. Good things that I *should* do, but mostly don't. Godly behaviors and misbehaviors. Rules I should be following. Most of us believers try to live by at least some of these rules and look down upon those who don't.

Indeed, we like rules, which, we tell ourselves without knowing it, make the work of God doable. Hence the *39 Melachot* of the rabbis—don't carry or light a fire or extinguish one or spin or weave or embroider or untangle—and the 39,000,000 unattainable holinesses stoutly held to by believers of all faiths. Feed the poor of the world. Free the imprisoned. Solve the problems of the needy.

---

*It appears that, in the time the Heidelberg Catechism was written, items in a list were followed by letters delineating the items, not preceded by them. Hence, here, "First, that the ministry of the gospel and the schools be maintained; (a) . . . and thus begin in this life the eternal sabbath. (g)"

We give ourselves no rest from these calls on our goodness. We modern-day Christians of every description, freed from the rule-driven life of Old Testament believers, nevertheless make up more rules for ourselves and ratchet up what Jesus identified as the two greatest commandments—love God and love others as ourselves—into ever heavier and more dreaded burdens, ever more impossible feats of faith.

That's the reality of such spiritual work assignments. We can't do them. We try and fail. Or we try and try and end up feeling bitter and burnt out and underappreciated. We misunderstand God's work as an unpleasant undertaking destined to fail, a summons to exertion that never abates.

Although we *are* called to be holy, this sort of exertion was not God's plan for us, nor does it win his love or approval. It only loads us down with more than we can carry and enslaves us to our guilt.

It was, in part, to address this problem that God sent his Son to our world. Not merely to model how holiness could be accomplished, if we were only perfect like Jesus, but to share with us the burden of God's holy work and thereby, with the same mysterious defiance of gravity of a child's grasp, to transform the old rules back into the shared experience of love God intended. Jesus came to free us from the stresses of both striving and failing. To invite us into God's welcoming arms for that promised rest.

25

Enjoying God's Bounty

Take delight in the LORD,
and he will give you the desires of your heart.

PSALM 37:4

ACTUALLY LOVING GOD BACK WITH all my heart, soul, strength, and mind is, for the literalist I tend to be, a vague undertaking at best.

First off, most of the loving I have done in my life has been unintentional. I could no more *not* love my daughters, for example, than not breathe. But while, as a matter of rhetoric, I might say I love them with my whole heart and soul and strength and mind—I might say, in other words, that I love them with every aspect of who I am—I have rarely actually set out to love them with any one of these parts of me. On occasion, I have had to expend what seemed like sheer strength to love my daughters, but I have never consciously said to myself, *Today I am going to love Charlotte with all my mind* or *Today my soul is Lulu's.* To be honest, I don't even really know how to differentiate my mind from my soul—or even from my heart, the metaphorical locus of my emotions.

Heart, mind, and soul are, insofar as I can conceptualize them at all, more or less the same organ: that impulse in me that responds and yearns, decides and initiates.

Loving God is problematic on another level. God is, after all, significantly unlike anyone else I have loved in my life. God is invisible, inaudible, intangible, and hard to really know in the same sense as I know—or at least think I know—others. Contrary to the teaching of certain songs sung in church these days, God cannot hold me or touch me and I can't see God's actual face. God doesn't have favorite meals I know about and can prepare and serve up. To visit God as I might a friend or a distant family member, I don't need to coordinate my schedule or buy an airplane ticket. God doesn't require diapering, as my daughters once did, or coddling, as they and my husband still do. God doesn't get sick and need taking care of. In sum, it is not possible to express love to God—and thus to intentionally set out to love God and know that I am doing so—in the same ways that I express love to my other loved ones.

So, coming to believe in God as an adult was not simultaneous, in my case, with coming to *love* God.

What does that really mean—*to love God?* I kept asking myself as a new believer.

My intuitive answer was to perform the love tasks suggested in church: namely, go to church, sing the songs, and dutifully follow the rules of Scripture as well as I could. And the performance of these love tasks occasionally moved me to something like the same sentiments I had for the humans I loved. Sometimes, the consideration of a concept in a sermon filled me with excitement, a sense of God's worthiness to be loved. Occasionally, a phrase in a hymn made me cry in recognition of God's love for such a pathetic believer as I am. Certainly, my reading of scriptural rules for holy behavior often made me conscious of my own unworthiness of God's love as well as of the wonderful gift of God's willingness to love me in spite of my failures. Every so often, my own conscious effort to do the right thing made me sense—or hope—that God might be pleased with me. But neither the performance of these love tasks nor their results ever made me *feel* as though I were loving God back.

"But loving God isn't about a *feeling*. It's about obedience," fellow believers told me, sending me back to those love tasks.

Here's the thing, though. Obeying is just not what I call loving. In fact, it's actually antithetical to it, at least as a motivation. Obedience often comes down to forcing myself to do something I don't want to do. Loving, on the other hand, is effortless and involuntary. In my closest relationships, love flows from me naturally. Certainly there have been moments in my love history when I had to force myself past fury or annoyance and back into a solid consciousness of my love for someone—even for my daughters, who began their existence as part of me and loving whom, as such, amounts to something akin to loving myself. Sometimes loving another is difficult. But—with my husband or daughters, for example—I am able to do it because love is already firmly established between us. I sense it there, and some part of me, despite my negative feelings, longs to return to it.

What ultimately taught me how to love God effortlessly, involuntarily, with my entire person, was reflecting on the two people of my acquaintance who, for a time, loved me that way: namely Charlotte and Lulu, back when they were little babies. Their love for me then comprised their entire existence and was entirely effortless, utterly involuntary. Their only love task could hardly be considered a task at all. All they were required to do was enjoy me and what I provided for them: the warmth of my arms around them, sweet sustenance from my body, the shelter and protection of home, and above all my company.

Their infantile enjoyment of me—their contentment in my presence, their insatiable hunger for the milk my body made for them, their obvious enthusiasm for whatever object I put before

them, their occasional smiles—constituted all the love I expected
or desired of them in return for my own. Only when they got older
did they start ignoring and sometimes even scorning these delights. But by then, as I say, our relationship was fully established
and we had developed habits of love expression—indeed, a whole
operation manual on how to love each other—to which we could
dutifully return to when things went awry.

An essential way of loving God, I learned by considering how
each of my infant daughters naturally went about loving me with
all of her little heart and soul and mind and strength, is simply to
enjoy God's many provisions to us: life, food, warmth, shelter,
protection, our lovely Earth and everything in it, one another, and,
most especially, God's own company.

So, I set out to consciously enjoy—even in moments of suffering—the life I had been given. Beginning with the created world
around me, I sought the palpable expression in my life of God's
invisible attributes: his love and amazing imagination and holy
habits. As a budding gardener, I enjoyed above all the soil, and I
gave myself over to that enjoyment as a key way of loving God. I
learned the names for all the weeds and flowers in our area, then
started watching birds. I rethought my existing enjoyment of food
and beauty and nature as intentional appreciations of God's provision. And I naturally—effortlessly, involuntarily—sought to
honor these provisions by sharing them, and my appreciation for
them, with my extended family, friends, students, and colleagues.

The more I enjoyed life, the more it seemed there was to enjoy.
The discovery reminded me of how I felt, once, as I neared the end
of a seemingly endless respiratory illness that coated my bronchial
tubes and sinuses with goo, when I began to recover my sense of
smell and taste. I called up my husband at work to report that I
had been able to smell the laundry that had just come out of the
dryer, then my deodorant, then the spaghetti sauce simmering on
the stove. I made bread that day and later on took a walk around

the yard, sniffing enthusiastically. Everything had a smell, I discovered, gorgeous and distinct, and my new consciousness of these boons overwhelmed me with gratitude.

And so I embarked on a life of thankfulness—eager to "give thanks in all circumstances," as Paul recommends in 1 Thessalonians 5:18—but I did so entirely by accident. As I became more aware of the delights of my daily existence, how could I *not* be thankful?

Even news of others' suffering—even my own suffering—often produced in me a paradoxical consciousness of the many other fortunes we enjoy as God's children, another source of thankfulness in my daily life. Conscious, intentional, guiltless enjoyment of God's creation has thus become a key medium through which I love God. When I enjoy what God created, I am unconsciously loving God with every part of me before I even know I'm doing it.

Setting out to enjoy creation also transformed how I interacted with God. In childhood, what I think of now as "prayer" had arisen spontaneously from an instinctive consciousness of God's presence, and I prayed a lot. In adulthood, by contrast, I struggled to remember and find time to pray, and even then my prayers felt one-sided, more along the lines of 911 calls—desperate pleas for help in my daily emergencies—than real interaction with someone I loved. I worked hard at trying to pray more effectively—less selfishly, more naturally, more enthusiastically. I listened closely on the rare occasion when fellow believers mentioned their own prayer habits, and I tried to emulate their practices. Still, I always felt that my own spotty communications with God were inadequate for a real relationship. I sought, and often received, comfort from God, but I never really talked about anything but my struggles and distress. To be honest, I never really "talked" to God at all beyond begging and whimpering.

Deciding to enjoy the created world amplified my awareness of God's constant company, though. I started to hear God's footsteps in my garden and, entirely without intending to, found myself commenting on this or that discovery and reflecting on the myriad ways nature expresses God and even humming little snatches of praise, not merely comforted by but comfortable in God's presence. Somehow, though I still wail forth my 911 prayers and certainly appreciate God's response, it's easier to feel genuine love for the One who made soil and little melon plants and rabbits, the living Person beside me as I walk between my raised beds in the morning, eager to find out what new plant or fruit has emerged overnight.

26

Helping Jesus Help Us

Jesus asked the boy's father,
"How long has he been like this?"

"From childhood," he answered. "It has often
thrown him into fire or water to kill him. But if you
can do anything, take pity on us and help us."

"'If you can'?" said Jesus. "Everything is
possible for one who believes."

Immediately the boy's father exclaimed,
"I do believe; help me overcome my unbelief!"

MARK 9:21–24

THE MOST IMPORTANT PRAYER ANYONE CAN PRAY is that of a man Jesus encounters who exclaims, "I believe; help my unbelief!" (Mark 9:24 NRSV).

This seemingly contradictory prayer is at once a declaration of faith and an admission of doubt. As such, it goes beyond the prayer

Jesus models for his disciples, which is essentially a credo framed as a plea: "I believe you are our Father, that your name is holy, that your plans will be carried out, that you provide for us and forgive our sins and protect us from evil." The believer who prays the Lord's Prayer is simply affirming the basic tenets of faith. The prayer "I believe; help my unbelief!" not only affirms faith—I believe!—but articulates the central dilemma of faith for many believers: we believe enough to *want* the impossibly good life God promises us but not enough to accept it.

Praying "I believe; help my unbelief!" also acknowledges the only solution to this dilemma: allowing God to solve even our failures of faith. In effect, the one who prays this prayer is depending on God to accomplish the only faith-assignment required of us: that is, believing in the One God Sent. As such, the story of the man who prayed this prayer is instructive.

The man's son, he tells Jesus in the exchange leading up to his prayer, "is possessed by a spirit that has robbed him of speech. Whenever it seizes him, it throws him to the ground. He foams at the mouth, gnashes his teeth and becomes rigid. I asked your disciples to drive out the spirit," he complains to Jesus, "but they could not" (Mark 9:17–18).

The man's faith-problem is manifold. Not only is a demon harming his son, but no experts in such matters—neither the teachers of the law present nor Jesus' own disciples—have succeeded in helping the boy. In addition, the crowd gathered around the man and his convulsing boy seems uninterested in their suffering. Instead of staying with the man and his boy, the disciples have gone off to argue with the rabbis about the matter, taking the nosy onlookers with them. The man is alone with his son when Jesus happens upon him.

The man's misery is surely overwhelming. His son has suffered this way from childhood, he tells Jesus. Luke's account adds that the boy is his only child. Plus, in those days, before preventive drugs or management strategies for seizures, there were no medical doctors who could offer an optimistic prognosis. There was nothing this father could do for his son besides move dangerous objects out of the way to keep him from getting hurt. The man has probably hoped before—some part of him hopes even as he addresses Jesus—but it has always come to nothing. Anyone who has ever hoped for a miraculous healing for an incurable illness knows what such doubt-fraught hope is like. So, even though this famous teacher does stop to ask what's wrong and the man is aware of Jesus' reputation as a healer, he is nevertheless wary, and his appeal echoes his reservations: "But if you can do anything," he hesitates, "take pity on us and help us" (Mark 9:22).

If there's one failing Jesus has little patience with, it's a puny faith, so he isn't very nice to the guy. First he admonishes him for prefacing his request with "if you can," then he tartly reminds him, "Everything is possible for one who believes" (Mark 9:23). This man's problems would already be solved if he merely had faith.

It is in response to Jesus' rebuke and impatient reminder that the man—surely despairing, his son writhing in the dirt at their feet—breaks down and wails, "I do believe; help me overcome my unbelief!" (Mark 9:24).

The man's prayer is sincere and raw and real, an uncontrived cry from within, like the prayers Paul describes in writing that believers "groan inwardly" (Romans 8:23) and even the Spirit "intercedes for us through wordless groans" (Romans 8:26).

This groan of a prayer is successful on so many levels. Unlike most prayers I have prayed, it has immediate and dramatic results. Jesus shakes his initial surliness and instantly commands what he disparages as "You deaf and mute spirit" not only to come out of the boy but to "never enter him again" (Mark 9:25). Then, we're told, the spirit "shrieked," convulsed the boy "violently" one last time, "and came out," leaving the boy, to all appearances, dead (Mark 9:26). The crowd rushes back to the scene of all this excitement just as Jesus takes the boy by the hand and helps him to his feet, and the boy finally stands in their midst—alive, healthy, and demon-free—surely curing his father's unbelief for good.

So much noise in this story! The rabbis and disciples arguing, Jesus rebuking, the rowdy crowd charging from drama to drama, the father crying out, and the "deaf and mute" spirit not only mysteriously hearing Jesus' words but somehow shrieking in response.

These last two noises—the father crying out, the demon shrieking—arc actually the same word in Greek: the onomatopoetic verb κράζω (krazō), literally the hoarse, emphatic caw of the raven. Matthew uses *krazō* to characterize Jesus' dying lament, "My God, my God, why have you forsaken me?" (Matthew 27:46). And John uses the same verb to capture Jesus' despairing exclamation to people who had seen "so many signs" but "still would not believe in him" (John 12:37). "I have come into the world as a light," Jesus cries out, "so that no one who believes in me should stay in darkness" (John 12:46).

And yet, we believers often *do* stay in darkness, a darkness of our own making. We remain as blind and deaf to what Jesus does and says, here and elsewhere, as that demon. So, when we hear Jesus' surprising promise, "Everything is possible for one who believes," we are just like that man in the story: We claim to believe this promise, but we can't really understand it, much less trust it as true.

The prayer "I believe; help my unbelief!" gets at the problem at the root of many unsuccessful prayers. So much of what we want in life—rest, ease, contentment, the assurance of our worthiness in God's eyes—seems impossible, despite God's promises. And when we want something impossible, as this boy's father does, it is so hard to believe that we can have it just for the asking.

Jesus says God is keen to "give good things to those who ask him!" (Matthew 7:11 NRSV). Nevertheless, when we pray for a seemingly impossible good thing, believing itself can seem impossible. In such situations, unbelief becomes an insurmountable and impenetrable wall between us and what we want, whether it's an improbable healing or some other immediate assistance from God or a more comprehensive end to the stresses, worries, guilts, and failures that consume our spirits. It is so tempting to seek out every other help besides God—experts, doctors, self-help books, our own holy efforts—that our trust in God and Scripture's promises ebbs from us. In impossible situations, believing itself takes effort, even for the holiest among us.

Belief takes, in other words, genuine exertion—especially today, when we can no longer see and touch Jesus, no longer actually hear his words. We live in a time when the miracles of Scripture seem like, well, miracles of Scripture: wonders of another time, another world, spectacular feats described in a book, not real-life events. Believing that we don't need to do anything for God, that Jesus really did accomplish everything, that nothing more difficult is required of us than that we ask, is hard work when all the evidence of our crippled world suggests that the fulfillment of God's promises is a gift of the future, not of now.

It is so tempting to discount God's favor that it takes what seems a fantastic effort to do otherwise. That despairing father's prayer for his son, for himself, bespeaks this effort and, as I have said, prescribes its remedy: We have to depend on God even for the one task we're asked to accomplish—faith itself.

That's what yoking oneself to the One God Sent entails: taking Jesus at his word that our part in what's expected of us will be easy. Our burden will be light. Our only job is to let Jesus groan and pull and exert himself to accomplish whatever it is we're supposed to accomplish, right down to believing itself.

Which is both harder and easier than it sounds.

When the disciples rejoin Jesus after the man's son is healed, they seem as vexed with themselves as the man had been at their failure to heal the boy. As soon as they can get Jesus off somewhere private, they ask, "Why couldn't we drive it out?" (Mark 9:28).

Jesus replied, "This kind can come out only by prayer" (Mark 9:29).

Such a simple answer, yet so confusing that theologians have debated it for millennia and some helpful translator in the Bible's history, determined to clarify the matter once and for all, even changed Jesus' response to read the way it is recorded in the King James Version: "This kind can come forth by nothing, but by prayer and fasting."

But there is no time for fasting in this rowdy story. And, whereas Jesus prays in most other instances in which he casts out demons or heals, he doesn't do so in any of the three Gospel accounts of this boy's restoration.

In fact, the only prayer the Gospel writers record is that desperate father's *krazō* of helplessness, unwittingly directed to the very One God Sent whose power he struggles to acknowledge: "I believe; help my unbelief!"

The verb *krazō*, I should have mentioned earlier, is also the same verb the apostle Paul uses to describe the ultimate prayer of helplessness. Those "who are led by the Spirit of God are the children of God," he explains. Not slaves cowering in fear but adopted children of God. "And by him we cry"— *krazō!*—"'*Abba*, Father'" (Romans 8:14–15).

This is all it takes to do God's work. Not a slavery of stress and guilt. Not fear of failure. Merely a willingness to cry out to God for help.

27

Loving the Poor in Spirit

Later Jesus found him at the temple and said to him,
"See, you are well again. Stop sinning or
something worse may happen to you."

JOHN 5:14

❧

I LOVE THE STORY OF THE GUY JESUS COMES UPON beside a pool where "a great number of disabled people used to lie—the blind, the lame, the paralyzed" (John 5:3). The guy is one of them. His disability is not specified, but whatever is wrong with him makes it difficult for him to get around, as he complains when Jesus asks him if he wants to get well: "I have no one to help me into the pool when the water is stirred. While I am trying to get in, someone else goes down ahead of me" (John 5:7).

Controversy abounds regarding this stirring of the waters. Some Bible translations, such as the King James Version, explain that "an angel went down at a certain season into the pool, and troubled the water: whosoever then first after the troubling of the water stepped in was made whole of whatsoever disease he had" (John 5:4 KJV). Contemporary scholars point out that these clarifications were not in the earliest versions of the Bible and posit that this stirring was a natural phenomenon: a periodic bubbling, like a geyser, that locals merely believed had curative powers.

Whatever the source of the water activity, it's this guy's crabby, fault-finding voice that interests me. Reading the account in John's Gospel, I'm certain John heard the man's whining with his own ears. I see the sick man in my mind, glaring at those he thinks ought to help him, gesturing accusingly at fellow sufferers who shove their way ahead of him into the pool. I imagine John thinking, as Jesus approaches the man, *Upon such a grumbler as this, Jesus' healing powers will be wasted.*

During the thirty-eight years the guy has been lying beside that pool, his disability, helplessness, loneliness, and others' derision have probably taken their toll on his likeability. Alongside his physical infirmity, he has acquired psychological ones. He's a complainer, a blamer, a quitter.

Jesus himself seems to find the guy rather hard to take. He responds curtly, "Get up! Pick up your mat and walk" (John 5:8) and, upon reencountering the guy, admonishes, "See, you are well again. Stop sinning or something worse may happen to you" (John 5:14). Even Jesus' initial question—"Do you want to get well?"— hints at exasperation. I mean, isn't it obvious that someone who's been lying by that pool for thirty-eight years *wants* to get well? In my mind, I always hear Jesus' question phrased in the negative— "Don't you want to get well?"—as though to suggest the guy's real infirmity is his bad attitude.

In other instances of healing, Jesus typically offers forgiveness before or in lieu of healing. While the lesson to be learned is surely that our spiritual wellness is more important than any bodily cure, it's nevertheless interesting to reflect that often, in suffering, we sin. We become self-focused and bitter. We complain. We worry about the future, about becoming a burden to others. Conversely, we often *make* ourselves into burdens through our negative emotions and desperate demands. In forgiving the sick, Jesus was perhaps forgiving such common but annoying reactions to suffering.

In any case, loving such people as that sick man by the pool—the angry, the blamers, the demanding, the irritating, the manipulative, the depressed, the mentally ill—takes special skills. In my experience, though I always want and intend to be understanding and kind to suffering loved ones, I often end up finding their attitudes and behaviors unbearable and my relationships with them so emotionally perilous that I end up reacting impatiently or else so superficially that it's as though we haven't interacted at all. After such an exchange, I am ashamed. Still, even as I make plans to be more loving in the future, I'm already dreading our next meeting. And when the time comes, I have to force myself to spend time with them. And so the cycle begins again. For me, loving the chronically miserable around me—the "poor in spirit," as I privately refer to them, using Jesus' mysterious term in Matthew 5:3—can be an especially heavy burden.

Before I continue—and alienate readers who would prefer to remain ignorant that their very suffering, which isn't their fault, can render them difficult to love—let me say that most of us are the poor in spirit at one time or another. I know I have been. Many times. As the result of a sexual assault when I was a college student, I have a mental illness that sometimes lands me in a strange state of combative self-isolation that taxes my loved ones. When I'm having an episode, I'm so claustrophobic I can't allow anyone to get close to me or, God forbid, touch me. Not even my husband. Not even my daughters back when they were innocent, cuddle-hungry toddlers. For weeks and sometimes months after my condition is triggered, unexpected movements or noises cause me to shriek and I easily fly into rages or crying fits.

My family and friends are admirably long-suffering, much more so than I might be if our roles were reversed. But once, during an extended episode, I asked a close friend why she didn't want to spend time with me, and she said: "You're no fun to be with anymore."

She was right. Miserable people are no fun to be with. They're typically self-focused, demanding, bitter, angry, pessimistic, and negative. Among the most love-needy in our acquaintance, they're often the hardest to love wholeheartedly. In response, many, like my friend, abandon the miserable to their misery.

The isolation of those who suffer has an interesting biological dimension. Recent studies on pain management have found that physical touch—whether massage or simply touching one's own hurt place—measurably reduces the perception of pain and releases hormones that relieve pain. Kissing a child's boo-boo, in other words, really can make it all better, and the laying on of hands actually can work on a purely physiological level. In theorizing about why this might be so, scientists speculate that touching an injury reverses an additional psychological pain that people in pain must often endure, which is that healthy people don't like to touch sick people. Jesus' many violations of this unspoken rule in his interactions with the infirm—in one instance he even sticks a wet finger in a man's ear!—are part of his own modus operandi as a lover of the poor in spirit.

Reexamining my own experiences in light of these sad truths about the variously poor in spirit has been, for me, transformative. How little it takes, it seems to me, to love those who are miserable and who, as a result, often seem so overwhelmingly difficult to love! A touch. A pat on the shoulder. The grasping of another's hand in greeting or prayer.

I have had unexpectedly pleasurable moments loving those I struggle to love simply by setting out to touch them at some point during a visit. I'm not a hugger by nature, so I have to consciously plan to touch others or it probably won't happen. Sometimes I even make up a pretext for doing so. I feel my mother-in-law's forehead to see if she's running a fever. I grab a disagreeable colleague's elbow in passing. And although it's probably illegal, or at least unprofessional, when a student enters my office distraught or angry about a grade—and thus not as lovable as usual—I make it my goal in that meeting to offer a pat on the arm or even, if the opportunity arises, to hug him or her.

It's become kind of a game for me to touch the untouchable. When I succeed, I feel as though I have won a prize, and often I have, since whoever it is usually interacts with me differently thereafter—less distrustfully, more lovingly—and thus becomes someone I no longer struggle as much to love. I'm happier with myself, then, and I sense God's approval.

Along the same lines, a cat-loving friend of mine once recommended, regarding a housebound relative's incessant appeals for company despite my long visits, that I "pet the cat"—that is, initiate small, regular contact *before* my relative demanded it. Such minimal input on my part, my friend said, would preempt such demands.

Truth be told, my friend's advice may work for cats (I know it doesn't for dogs, since if I so much as touch Moe-dog's head in passing, he'll trot after me all day long), but it didn't work for my housebound relative. She called several times after every visit to thank me and recount everything she'd been up to after we'd last spoken.

That said, the experiment helped me discover another way of petting the cat that pleases both my relative and me and averts the resentment I used to feel after a visit had left her unsatisfied. Since my relative loves homemade bread and I'm always baking it, I make her a little loaf whenever I bake and drop it by her house on my way to work or to run errands. I never call in advance, and the fact that I'm on my way somewhere else automatically limits our interaction to a short, enjoyable exchange. The little loaf itself extends the visit, after

I say good-bye, for the day or two it takes her to consume it. Baking an extra loaf costs me minimal effort and pleases her immensely—not just the bread and the visit but being able to brag about both to her friends. It gratifies me as well, since she can't say enough about how good the bread is. I've since baked bread for friends laid low by illness and to repair relationships strained by conflict.

Not everyone adores bread, though—not even sourdough bread still warm from the oven. For these, I remember the training of my sister Sharon, a nurse who works with the mentally ill. Nurses set clear boundaries, she says, to benefit their patients as well as themselves. To preempt someone wanting more from me than I can give—more time, more help, more attention, more patience—I decide in advance exactly how I can be most concretely useful to the person and then set out to do just that one thing.

You may need to consult with the disheartened person, as I had to in the case of a depressed friend who struggles with suicidal thoughts and often goes missing for long periods of time, before you light on the right small thing. After one of my friend's episodes, during which I left many frantic messages on his phone machine begging him to return my call, he pointed out that my efforts only compounded his misery.

"I need to hear from people," he explained, "but I just can't answer the phone when I'm like that, so then I have to feel bad about that too."

We came up with the strategy of my sending "thinking of you" greeting cards to remind him that he is loved.

Aiming small is key to easing the burden of loving those who are difficult to love. With the goal of transforming your love from a duty into something pleasurable, select one tiny act of love, the smaller and more concrete the better, and then carry it through. You will be surprised about how much better not only *you* feel about your efforts afterward but also the person you are helping. And, if you let yourself, you will sense God's pleasure.

28

The Secret of Being Content

*I have learned the secret of being content in any
and every situation, whether well fed or hungry,
whether living in plenty or in want.*

PHILIPPIANS 4:12

MY PARENTS RECENTLY TOOK AN ELDERHOSTEL TRIP to the
Badlands of South Dakota. Not my kind of vacation: a long-distance
bus trip with a bunch of cheery strangers, guided tours, outdoor
lectures in the summer heat, the whole question mark of a place
that would be South Dakota in my imagination. Afterward, my
dad called to rave about all they'd seen and learned about: the
Lakota Sioux, Mount Rushmore, a woolly mammoth excavation
site so authentic someone could have just gone over to the pile of
ancient bones and stolen one. (He didn't.)

When my stepmother called a few days later, she said nothing
about these delights. South Dakota had affected her on a deeper
level.

"A few days into the trip, I just felt so calm and good," she told me. "Something about the place opened me. I don't know when I've ever felt so content."

Contentment is elusive for most of us. Enter "contentment" or "happiness" into the search box at Amazon.com, and you'll be presented with tens of thousands of titles. One title—*Stumbling on Happiness*—encapsulates our tendency to view contentment as something momentous and rare, not easily attained or permanently available. Contentment is out there somewhere, we hope— perhaps in the South Dakota Badlands—but finding it is a matter of chance. We might flirt with the idea that it can be constructively pursued and perhaps buy a how-to-be-happy book and stumble forth in search of it. Deep down, though, we suspect contentment cannot be had—or, if so, only in glimpses. Certainly it's not available here, now, and always.

That's how I regarded my own contentment early in my marriage, anyway. I loved my husband, and our life together satisfied longings I'd amassed in my years living alone in foreign cities: for children, furniture, nature, a big kitchen, home. I gave up much for these boons. On our farm, Europe and China, friends and family, were far behind me. I missed the metropolitan life, not least such delicacies unattainable in Oklahoma as lamb, decent bread, and Lapsang Souchong tea.

Marriage also burdened me with new responsibilities: cars, water heaters, a lawn needing mowed at least once a week throughout summer and fall, an elderly mother-in-law involved in everything my family did. I was happily married. But I certainly wasn't happy all the time.

Increasingly, I saw happiness as everything I had given up— thrilling experiences, distant friends, freedom to leave whenever I wanted—plus an escape from new burdens that accrued as the girls got older and Kris and I moved out of farming into other jobs. Contentment, in short, was somewhere else, and I fantasized often about this imagined other place: a romanticized version of those lonely years abroad conflated with a stress-free future I could envision only indistinctly, a dim brightness just beyond the horizon. My fantasy was akin to, if not synonymous with, my fuzzy understanding of heaven. The Bible, I was learning, had surprisingly little to say about heaven—little, that is, about what *I* wanted to know: namely, what it would be like to live there.

In the Old Testament, "heaven" is primarily presented not as the afterlife but as what's above us, where God lives. Devout Israelites who died rested—in what I hoped was a metaphor—with their fathers.

The New Testament added little besides the scary-sounding depictions of heaven—again, hopefully metaphorical—in Revelation. Many of Jesus' parables do begin with the words, "The kingdom of heaven is like . . ." but what invariably follows seems very much from this world: a tiny mustard seed growing into the biggest garden vegetable, yeast worked into dough, treasure hidden in a field, a merchant looking for fine pearls—each story a manifestation, it seemed to me, of hope itself more than anything else.

A concrete biblical depiction of the happy afterlife Christians believe in was as elusive as contentment in this life. Indeed, as Jesus tells Nicodemus, "No one has ever gone into heaven except the one who came from heaven—the Son of Man" (John 3:13). End of story.

The good news is that, according to both Old Testament and New, contentment in this life is attainable. And not just in glimpses or just in South Dakota. It's available to us constantly and everywhere. Solomon promises, "The fear of the LORD leads to life; then one rests content, untouched by trouble" (Proverbs 19:23), and Paul, writing from prison, confirms Solomon's promise: "I have learned the secret of being content in any and every situation, whether well fed or hungry, whether living in plenty or in want. I can do all this through him who gives me strength" (Philippians 4:12–13).

Paul makes several important points about contentment here. First, it's a secret known to few. Second, it's attainable in the most miserable of circumstances. Third, being happy is something we "do"—something that takes effort and strength—not something that happens to us. Finally, the strength that enables contentment comes from God, who evidently wants us to be happy.

That's, strangely, a hard place to get to—that God wants us to be happy. As a child, I believed just the opposite. I equated holiness with sacrifice and admired those who gave up everything to help others or risked their health to live among lepers. I'm not questioning the value of such sacrifices here, merely trying to tap the underpinnings of my admiration for them: I believed suffering pleased God.

Reading the Bible as a new parent, though, I discovered God's desires to be much like my own for my children. I wanted them to be happy. Like the father in Jesus' parable who, though nowhere near death, divvies out an inheritance to his greedy son, I often found myself letting my children have whatever they wanted, even things I thought they shouldn't have. God was no different.

"Which of you, if your son asks for bread, will give him a stone? Or if he asks for a fish, will give him a snake?" Jesus asks. "If you, then, though you are evil, know how to give good gifts to your children, how much more will your Father in heaven give good gifts to those who ask him!" (Matthew 7:9–11).

Jesus makes these promises to crowds of sufferers who have pursued him great distances hoping for the same contentment we all want. And surely contentment is the best gift God could give us.

Fast-forward a dozen years into my increasingly hectic and malcontented life. Kris was a CPA by then and I a professor, our daughters teenagers with diverse activities pulling us in every direction, my yearnings earlier in marriage receding to vague reminiscence, faded photographs in a dusty shoe box.

That year I went on sabbatical and wrote, full-time, at home. I set up a desk in the living room, between two windows looking out past the front porch to the yard and beyond that the pastures where our cows once grazed and Kris and I once hayed every summer. The fields were now leased to a neighbor for his cattle and hay. I spent that year watching others do the hard work my husband and I used to do—easy work in my memory, compared to teaching—while I sat at my desk and reflected and wrote.

Much was good about my life then. Kris and I got along. Our girls were thriving. We lived in a house built to my specifications. I loved my job. Nevertheless, I still mourned my apartment in Berlin, street markets, art museums, the neighborhood bakery that sold double-crusted rye loaves—and I forgot the loneliness and dissatisfaction that accompanied these delights. Although I rarely mentioned my longings to Kris or anyone else, deep down I was still bitter for having given up my entire history and every relationship that was ever important to me for our puny life on a remote Oklahoma farm, while Kris had stayed right where he wanted to be when we married: on the comforting chunk of land he'd known from childhood, with his mom nearby, at home in every sense of the word and utterly content.

From the windows flanking my desk, I looked out over this home. At the pasture changing seasons and the deer sneaking out of the shadowy woods to graze at morning, then disappear, then reemerge as the afternoon melted into night. I grew my first garden that year and learned to recognize the songbirds. And slowly, slowly, I started to appreciate the amazing fortune of being where I was.

Sheer rest was part of it—a literal Sabbath-rest coming on the heels of six frenzied years of working and child-rearing simultaneously, racing home to pick up the girls and take them to lessons and ball games and put them to bed and somewhere in between get a meal cooked and essays graded and the house picked up enough to disguise its underlying grubbiness for another day.

During my sabbatical, my days settled into a new, restful order. As soon as my family left for school or work, I washed the breakfast dishes, started bread dough or a pot of beans, then took a walk through my garden or the woods before settling in to write. After a midday break, I sat back down to work. And all the while the cardinals whistled from the trees, and the sun or rain beat down, and seeds floated on the wind.

Although I worked hard during my seventh-year rest, it seemed a lazy year, a strangely time-stopping passage of time I remember primarily as a series of sensory discoveries. Bird voices. The smell of morning. How melon seedlings broke the dirt and spread out their leaves, like sturdy little human children, their arms outstretched in play. I had never paid such close attention before to the world around me.

But it wasn't merely rest that taught me contentment. Nor was it the beauty of the Ozarks. I learned, that year, to quit gazing backward or forward and recognize where I was right now as my promised land.

Every time I embark on daily Bible-reading, I always begin at the beginning and never get much past Deuteronomy before, in my busyness, abandoning the habit. After such biblical forays, the stories of Moses and the Israelites dithering in the desert instead of progressing into the Promised Land always linger in my consciousness.

Like me, the Israelites pined for the past—ironically, in their case, a past when they were slaves, toiling as bricklayers and being punished for daring to ask for a holiday. They disparaged even the tasty-sounding manna—like "wafers made with honey" (Exodus 16:31) or "something made with olive oil" (Numbers 11:8)—with which God kept them from starvation and wailed, "If only we had meat to eat! We remember the fish we ate in Egypt at no cost—also the cucumbers, melons, leeks, onions and garlic. But now we have lost our appetite; we never see anything but this manna!" (Numbers 11:4–6).

At God's urging, they sent out scouts to see if this promised homeplace really was so wonderful, and the scouts returned "bearing a single cluster of grapes" so massive that "two of them carried it on a pole between them, along with some pomegranates and figs" (Numbers 13:23). They brought also terrifying reports of difficulties they were sure they'd encounter there: powerful people occupying hills, coastline, even desert, in cities "fortified and very large" (Numbers 13:28). "The land we explored devours those living in it," they concluded (Numbers 13:32).

That year, I came to recognize myself in those Israelites, pining for the past and worrying about the future, and took especially to heart God's admonition to them, after their return to Mount Sinai, the site of their earlier appointments with God: "You have stayed long enough at this mountain," he said. "See, I have given you this land. Go in and take possession of the land the LORD swore he would give to your fathers" (Deuteronomy 1:6, 8).

During my sabbatical, I left my mountain of longing and entered my promised land—the literal land, but more generally the life in which I found myself. Married to a man who loved me, with daughters soon to embark on lives of their own and fulfilling work as a teacher and writer. Throughout the year, I surveyed the delights of my current life and decided I had stayed long enough at my mountain of dissatisfactions. Then, having decided—and it took a mindful decision to give up my reminiscences of a different past and fantasies of a better future—I advanced into my present life as never before and took possession of it. I have never regretted it.

Often I reflect that, just as people can be categorized by learning styles (visual, auditory, kinesthetic) and relational habits (introverts and extroverts, leaders and followers), most can be located principally in one of the three main tenses: past, present or future. Some people I know have astonishingly rich memory lives. They speak of dead relatives with interest and strong emotion, whether fondness or grief or bitterness. Often I envy such people's ability to remember, decades and even half centuries later, specific incidents, details, turns of phrase. They send out masses of Christmas cards and commemorate not only births but deaths and anniversaries with special meals and rituals.

Others I know constantly look ahead. They love planning, budgeting, saving up. They're always talking about the next step in their career, their hopes or fears for their children, what they will do if this or that happens. They wield the video camera at family celebrations and employee gatherings and they plan their retirements while still in their forties.

The ones who live in the present don't talk about their life much. Not past, not future, not even present. They're too occupied with living it, enjoying it.

I languish in each tense from time to time. Each has its pleasures. But it is in the last tense that I find myself the happiest.

We each have a promised land—the very life we are living. Our promised land is, simply, the place where we are, both physically and metaphorically. Like the Israelites in the desert, though, we often hesitate to enter it. We perceive its potentialities as uninviting, even dangerous. And yet, it is here where our contentment lies, where God's work awaits us.

29

What My Dogs Know

The Gospel of Rest

Are you so foolish? After beginning with the Spirit,
are you now trying to attain your goal by human effort?

GALATIANS 3:3 NIV 1984

EVER SINCE MY SABBATICAL, I have been trying to decide whether or not to quit my teaching job and devote myself exclusively to writing. It should be an easy decision. Even with both daughters in college, I find that working two demanding jobs—teaching and writing—just isn't working: I do neither job as well as I want to, and I feel frantic all the time. But giving up a regular paycheck seems impossible. Just thinking about it makes potential disasters loom on my mental horizon.

It's not that I don't like my job. On the contrary, I love teaching and interacting with students and colleagues. Even going to meetings. Even, if I am not under stress, grading papers. But I am usually under stress, I discovered. It took the experience of rest to make me recognize its opposite.

During my sabbatical, I discovered thirsts I never knew I had—for weather, birds, certain kinds of light, certain times of day. The dawn is pink for five minutes each morning. Ten, sometimes, with the right kind of clouds. Even though I've always gotten up early enough to see it, I rarely noticed it before my sabbatical. Time, I learned, was like rain or sunlight or pink or birdsongs. They came and did their good and then were gone, and, although I spent many hours each day hard at work writing, I drank deeply from these divine gifts.

During that year, in contrast to my entire previous work-life, I ate lunch daily. Outside, if it was nice weather. A salad fresh-picked from my garden, most times, dressed with the merest teaspoon of olive oil, a scattering of salt and sugar, and vinegar. I could see our dogs in the outer reaches of the yard, lounging in the sun.

"Here, Tessi! Here, Erica! Moe-dog, come here!" I called. But they just lay there. Or loitered a bit nearer to the picnic table and dozed off again.

Who knew that dogs spent their days sleeping? All the aphorisms say so, of course—a dog's life, let sleeping dogs lie. Before that year, though, I knew our dogs only in attitudes of frenzy. Jumping up at me. Wanting to be fed. Tripping me in their excitement at getting to accompany me to the mailbox. In my year at home, I learned the secret of their perpetual good nature, and it is this: Dogs spend their days AND their nights at rest. They live, I have come to think, as God would have humans live. Stress-free. Guilt-free. Worry-free. Not waking at 3:23 A.M. to fantasize about terminal diseases but at peace with the world, saving their frenzies for something worthwhile. For fellowship. Food. A walk in the sun.

Kris and I have been reading Isaiah. It's a grim book, mostly, and hard to enter first thing in the morning: a list of bad things that will happen to this people or that, and presumably to us, if we don't live the way God wants us to.

For the first twenty chapters or so, I understood this living right as the usual sort promoted in Scripture. No worshiping of idols or intermarrying with idol-worshiping foreigners. No abusing widows or robbing the fatherless. No being "heroes at drinking wine and champions at mixing drinks" (Isaiah 5:22—it's really in there!).

Despite the modern-day sound of some of Isaiah's images, I found it hard to get convicted by anything the prophet said. This was nothing new, though. Isaiah's contemporaneous listeners had the same problem. Even after Isaiah took to preaching in the nude, which you'd think would make anyone perk up and pay attention, his listeners just mocked him.

To try and make the prophet's words more applicable to our own lives and interests, Kris and I talked about the farming practices of those times and about Isaiah's famous prophecy that "The virgin will conceive and give birth to a son, and will call him Immanuel" (7:14). He's clearly speaking of Jesus, we decided, although our study Bible's notes suggested Isaiah may have meant his own virgin wife and their child.

Driving to school one morning, I tried to make Isaiah's grim predictions more personal to my own life by composing new chapters in my head:

> An oracle concerning Westville, Oklahoma, that Patty Kirk
> saw:
> Woe to you people of the eastern Arkansas!
> See, the LORD rides on a swift cloud and is coming to
> Westville, even to you in
> Siloam Springs, to you, John Brown University!
> Highway 412 stands desolate, the parking lots empty and
> cracking, the stores in ruins, their shelves of
> merchandise crushed to pieces.
> The idols of the Ozarks tremble before him!

It was fun, but it didn't really move me. I hate when that happens with Scripture. I feel gypped. I mean, here I was reading what I knew I should be reading at 6:00 A.M., and I found it less gripping than *Time* magazine or the latest Williams-Sonoma catalog.

Then Kris and I got to this electrifying passage where Isaiah's listeners were mocking him, babbling his words back to him like little children in meaningless-sounding streams:

> "Do and do, do and do,
>> rule on rule, rule on rule;
>> a little here, a little there." (Isaiah 28:10 NIV 1984)

In Hebrew, the jumble of words sounds even more mocking, like the meaningless noises we use to mimic a fool—*blah blah blah*—which is precisely what some scholars think Isaiah is recording in this passage:

> *ṣaw lāṣāw ṣaw lāṣāw*
> *qaw lāqāw qaw lāqāw*

The passage is evidently difficult to decipher, as different versions come up with wildly dissimilar translations, but Isaiah's response to his listeners' mockery clears it all up, to my view. "Very well then," he tells them,

> with foreign lips and strange tongues
>> God will speak to this people,
>> to whom he said,
>> "This is the resting place, let the weary rest";
>> and, "This is the place of repose"—
>> but they would not listen.
>> So then, the word of the LORD to them will become:
>>> Do and do, do and do,
>>> rule on rule, rule on rule;
>>> a little here, a little there—
>> so that they will go and fall backward,
>> be injured and snared and captured. (Isaiah 28:11–13
>> NIV 1984)

Here was genuine prophecy. Having rejected God's offer of rest and repose, we do and do, create rule upon rule, add a few more tasks here and there, until we are used up and ensnared in a web of doing. In lunging forward, we fall backward. Our best attempts to grasp God's promised place of repose become garbled dreams of languishing in a hospital bed. And then death, the ultimate rest.

Later that day, I listened to a classical music program on the radio. The host recounted the story of Roger Tapping, violist of one of the world's best string quartets. In 2003, the group won a Grammy for "Best Chamber Music Performance" and went on tour.

It was probably Tapping's one chance at fame as a chamber musician, but his family was unhappy. I have a brother who's a rock musician and on the road a lot, so I know how hard that kind of life can be on a family—which is probably not much different from how hard Kris's tax season is on my family. In any case, Tapping's family offered him an ultimatum: It's us or the quartet. And, to what was clearly the host's—and my— amazement, the man quit. It was, according to Tapping, the hardest decision of his life. And the best.

And so I'm back to my own decision about whether or not to quit one of my jobs. Why is it so difficult, this business of choosing family and health and happiness over stress and guilt? Why is the decision to work less, strive less, suffer less—to rest—so hard for many of us to make?

Our habitual striving infects every aspect of our lives, I think, rendering even ardent believers incapable of understanding God's invitation in Isaiah—"This is the resting place; let the weary rest!" In fact, we hear the words as their opposite, weighing ourselves and one another down with seemingly essential spiritual tasks, starting with church attendance and charity and mushrooming into a willingness to do all things called "Christian." Even though we know our salvation comes exclusively from God and cannot be achieved through our own efforts, many of us believers are nevertheless secretly worried we don't pray well enough or avoid enough sins or do enough good. We long to be "purpose-driven"—if the success of the bestselling books by that name is any measure—but don't realize that we already *are*. Driven. And, as a consequence, crippled by stress. And, when our best intentions fail, as they inevitably will, by guilt.

Throughout Scripture, God proffers rest, promising Moses, "My Presence will go with you, and I will give you rest" (Exodus 33:14) and, speaking through Joshua, "The LORD your God will give you rest" (Joshua 1:13). David rhetorically questions the Israelite leaders, "Is not the LORD your God with you? And has he not granted you rest on every side?" (1 Chronicles 22:18). Jesus preaches, "Come to me, all you who are weary and burdened, and I will give you rest" (Matthew 11:28). Even the spiritual workaholic Paul chides, "Are you so foolish? After beginning with the Spirit, are you now trying to attain your goal by human effort?" (Galatians 3:3 NIV 1984).

Rest. I have never heard this gospel—and it is such good news!— preached. Instead, we believers wield biblical mandates at one another and ourselves like weapons—Do and do! Rule upon rule!— and relegate Scripture's repeated promises of rest and contentment to an afterlife we can't even imagine. Like Isaiah's contemporaries—like me, in my reluctance to reduce my oppressive workload—we enter "a covenant with death" through our pious exertion, inwardly boasting, as Isaiah accuses his listeners of boasting, "When an overwhelming scourge sweeps by, it cannot touch us" (Isaiah 28:15).

Driven, and tragically mistaken in our belief that our drivenness is the holy work God demands, we miss out altogether on the restful contentment that is the believer's chief spiritual reward, in this world *and* the next.

30

Walking on Water

Shortly before dawn Jesus went out to them, walking on the lake. When the disciples saw him walking on the lake, they were terrified. "It's a ghost," they said, and cried out in fear.

But Jesus immediately said to them:
"Take courage! It is I. Don't be afraid."

"Lord, if it's you," Peter replied,
"tell me to come to you on the water."

"Come," he said.

Then Peter got down out of the boat,
walked on the water and came toward Jesus.

MATTHEW 14:25–29

I LOVE THE STORIES OF PETER IN THE BIBLE. No one else of Jesus' companions loves him as enthusiastically, telling Jesus, "not just my feet but my hands and my head as well!" after Jesus says, "Unless I wash you, you have no part with me" (John 13:8–9).

On another occasion, Jesus takes Peter, James, and John up on a high mountain, where he metamorphoses into a dazzling, otherworldly version of himself, his face shining "like the sun" (Matthew 17:2) and his clothes turning "whiter than anyone in the world could bleach them" (Mark 9:3). Jesus is joined on the mountaintop by the centuries-dead prophets Moses and Elijah, and the disciples, especially Peter, "did not know what to say, they were so frightened" (Mark 9:6). Nevertheless, the events clearly call for some sort of holy response, so Peter blurts out, comically, "Rabbi, it is good for us to be here. Let us put up three shelters—one for you, one for Moses and one for Elijah" (Mark 9:5). Peter, more than any other disciple—except perhaps that woman who poured perfume onto Jesus' head—never stops to think what he *should* be doing or saying in a given moment but instead acts spontaneously, usually inspired by the holiest of all motivations, love.

No one else's faith crashes as categorically and famously as Peter's does, though, when he pretends not to know Jesus on the day leading up to the crucifixion. Whenever I hear a rooster crow—which is fairly often out in the country where I live—I think of Peter's astonishing failure, in that moment of denial, to do the one simple task God asks of us all, believing in the One God Sent, and I am reassured anew that, even if I fail, as I am bound to do, God will not abandon me and that the One God Sent himself will nevertheless make good on his offer to share his yoke with me and pull me clear. If Peter is salvageable after failing Jesus so spectacularly, I reason, then maybe I am too.

My favorite Peter stories, however, are his breathtaking moments of faith. When Jesus asks his disciples who they think he is, they offer a series of secondhand guesses: "They replied, 'Some say John the Baptist; others say Elijah; and still others, Jeremiah or one of the prophets'" (Matthew 16:14). Alone among them, Peter answers confidently and directly, supplying a hard-to-believe truth he must have heard—and believed—from Jesus' own lips: "You are the Messiah, the Son of the living God" (Matthew 16:16).

The very best Peter story is when he walks on water, though. I have yet to hear a sermon on this amazing feat of faith that does not either diminish it in light of Peter's failure a few moments later, when he "saw the wind" and sank (Matthew 14:30), or else focus our attention on *Jesus'* ability to walk on water instead of Peter's. And, though countless artists from the medieval times onward have depicted this story, I have yet to discover a single painting showing not only Jesus but Peter confidently pacing the waves. If Peter is shown at all, he is sinking, flailing in a vain effort to stay afloat, or else being pulled up. My Bible's subheadings label the story "Jesus Walks on the Water," making no mention whatsoever of Peter.

For me, though, this story is all about Peter. In the beginning of the story, Peter's with the other disciples, whom Jesus has sent away so that he can go off by himself and pray. They're in a boat "already a considerable distance from land, buffeted by the waves because the wind was against it" (Matthew 14:24). Night falls, and evidently they keep on fishing or else the headwind makes it impossible for them to row back to shore. Or maybe they just keep on floating out there on the water because they don't know what to do in Jesus' absence and are afraid something has happened to him that he's taking so long.

In any case, Jesus does eventually return to them, not waiting for them to join him but going "out to them, walking on the lake" (Matthew 14:25). They are, understandably "terrified": "'It's a ghost,' they said, and cried out in fear" (Matthew 14:26).

Jesus tries to reassure them by identifying himself and telling them, "Don't be afraid" (Matthew 14:27).

Then, though, Peter does something peculiar: "Lord, if it's you," Peter replied, "tell me to come to you on the water" (Matthew 14:28). Apparently unfazed by Jesus' magic trick of walking around on the wind-buffeted lake, he offers to join him. He speaks in the imperative here, commanding Jesus to command *him* to do the impossible, but the audacity of this command—giving orders to God's own Son—is profoundly faithful.

Command me to believe, he is, in effect, saying, and I will. I can do this work you want of me, this business of believing in the One God Sent, but only with your help.

And Jesus acquiesces, saying, simply, "Come" (Matthew 14:29).

So Peter steps out of the boat onto the lake.

Just like that.

When I consider what that moment might have been like from Peter's perspective, I imagine the wind-tossed water feeling something like Jell-O beneath my feet. Or, like a hillside stream near our house in Connecticut that froze during a cold snap not long after we moved there, its splashing and movement and sprays hardening overnight into slippery bumps and knobs and sharp crests of white ice.

Surely Peter walked gingerly, feeling his way along, aware that the surface might collapse at any moment and yet confident that it wouldn't. For a moment, he steadied himself on that new surface, seeking balance before directing his feet and weight and attention toward the familiar voice and form of the one he knew and loved and revered above all others. The Messiah. The Son of the living God.

Moments later, when Peter does, alas, notice again the wind and the waves and remember to be afraid, he has already progressed so far toward his goal that he is close enough for Jesus to simply reach out his hand and catch him, lamenting, "You of little faith . . . why did you doubt?" (Matthew 14:31).

And that is it. The story of Peter's walk of faith. His faith is small, to be sure. Only big enough to carry him a few footsteps in Jesus' direction, but a little faith is better than none at all. And to me, this demonstration of Peter's miniscule faith is the best example in the entire Bible of the work of God—of genuinely believing in the One God Sent, believing enough to walk on water, if only for a second or two—and it is the kind of work I want to emulate.

In some sense, it is difficult. Scary. Gutsy. Weird. But breaking it down into its several parts encourages me somewhat.

First, to dare to command the One God Sent to call me to himself.

Then, when he does call me toward him—and he will, since he makes promises along these lines again and again in Scripture—to step out of my scary little boat onto the strange, firm, otherworldly water of faith.

To revel in that moment. Surely Peter did.

And then, when I notice the waves and remember my earlier fears and start to sink back into the reality of the lesser world I usually live in, to cry out, as Peter does, "Lord, save me!" (Matthew 14:30) and feel the hand of the One God Sent grab mine and pull me back up.

Demand to be called. Step out. Enjoy it as long as I can. And then, inevitably, surrender myself to my own frailty and the strong arm of the One God Sent. That's what it is to do God's work. It's that carefree. That effortless. That delightful.

IVP *Crescendo*
COURAGE. CONFIDENCE. CALLING.

Some voices challenge us. Others support or encourage us. Voices can move us to change our minds, draw close to God, discover a new spiritual gift. The voices of others are shaping who we are.

The voices behind IVP Crescendo join together to draw us into God's story. We'll discover God's work around the globe even as we learn to love the people around the corner. We'll have opportunity to heal our places of pain. We'll discover new ways to love our families. We'll hear God's voice speaking into our lives as we discover new places of influence.

IVP Crescendo invites you to join in the rising chorus

- *to listen to the voices of others*
- *to hear the voice of God*
- *and to grow your own voice in*

COURAGE. CONFIDENCE. CALLING.

---

ivpress.com/crescendo
ivpress.com/crescendo-social